Memories of a Japanese Doctor in Baltimore

Sixty Years in My Adopted Home

by

Hiroshi Nakazawa

ISBN: 9781704756127

Cover and Interior Book Design by Shannon Cate Editing
shannoncate.online

Introduction

This is the story of a Japanese surgeon who moved to America at a young age shortly after World War II. He overcame many struggles and challenges to survive and become a good citizen and leader in his local community. Dr. Hiroshi Nakazawa still lives in Baltimore in good health, surrounded by his wife and other family members, and remains active in his field.

Dr. Nakazawa spent the war years as a child in Japan. He intended to take over the family's medical business, so he entered Chiba University's School of Medicine after the war. He took the intern examination at the US Naval Hospital in Yokosuka, using the Southern accented English he had learned from American movies. This was the start of a long relationship with the United States and was the beginning of his second life. His circumstances during this time demonstrate the inspiration he would need to overcome the turbulence of American society, where he would spend most of his life, and his courage to act.

After moving to the US, Dr. Nakazawa's roles included practicing surgeon, President of the Baltimore City

Medical Society, President of the St. Agnes Hospital Doctors Association, and Vice Chair of the Maryland Medical Society. As a community-based Japanese physician, his achievements are unparalleled. Recognized in a highly competitive meritocracy, he became a respected figure, a so-called "self-made man." So this is also a sweat and tear-streaked battle story.

But at the same time, he reveals mistakes he made, setbacks he experienced during this time, and how he learned from these mistakes. He also talks about his experience with the open-mindedness of Americans. He expresses gratitude to those who encouraged and supported him, in particular, to his wife Mineko, who "acts American on the outside and sticks to the American way of thinking but who retains the old ways like a Japanese person." His wife is the guiding force of his life.

Individual stories cannot be told independent of the surrounding society and the circumstances and spirit of the times. Dr. Nakazawa's story is no exception.

The Pacific War had a huge impact on his parents and family as it did on the majority of Japanese at the time. The young Dr. Nakazawa, who struggled to attain an education and took the risk of a lifetime by moving to the US, met and married Mineko, a Sansei, in Baltimore. Mineko, like many other Japanese-Americans, was called a Jap during the war and treated horribly. Even now, more than 70 years after the end of the war, the emotional scars remain from the war between Japan, her family's homeland, and the United States, her country. Political and diplomatic reconciliations and pledges may offer comfort to the wounded, but they cannot erase painful memories.

Along with his activities as a local medical association leader, Dr. Nakazawa strives to strengthen the sister-city relationship between Kawasaki and Baltimore. He has promoted grassroots exchange in his role as Chairman of the Baltimore-Kawasaki City Sister City Committee. The strong ties between the US and Japan and the warm friendship between the whole US nation and non-partisan Japan are supported by the efforts of many individuals like Dr. Nakazawa.

During my time as ambassador to the US, I enjoyed a friendship with Dr. and Mrs. Nakazawa. By then, the doctor had spread his wings to expand his practice from general surgery to Eastern medicine and acupuncture. Whenever I saw him at receptions, he would say to me, "How are you feeling? Acupuncture is really effective." Simply hearing these words would send a warm breeze through my heart and leave me feeling as if I had received acupuncture.

At the end of his story, he has a message for Japanese people, especially young people. "I feel that unless you make an effort to go somewhere else, breath the air there, come to know the people around you and learn, Japan will be left behind again in the future." All in all, I agree.

December 2018, Tokyo

Kenichiro Sasae

(Former Japanese Ambassador to the United States)

Chapter One

My Childhood and Life in Takasaki

I was born in Takasaki, Gunma Prefecture in 1932. My father was born in 1895, a year after the sudden outbreak of the First Sino-Japanese War, and my mother in 1904, the year of the Russo-Japanese War. Although the Treaty of Portsmouth was concluded the subsequent year, anti-Japanese sentiment emerged and spread in the US around this time. World War I broke out in 1914, and despite being a victorious country, Japan was never treated as an equal of the "first-class" powers—such as Great Britain or the United States— and this led to growing dissatisfaction among Japanese citizens. In 1924, US President Wilson signed the Immigration Act of 1924, which banned immigration from Japan to the United States, causing opposition in Japan to US racial discrimination.

My sister had been born in 1930, when Japan was initiating a military operation into Manchuria. The following year (1931), the Manchurian Incident occurred, and my father was sent to the battlefield. Around the time I was born, the relationship between Japan and China was worsening, and in 1937, when I was five years old, the Second Sino-Japanese War broke out. At the Takasaki Station, more and more infantrymen of the 15th regiment were sent away amidst shouts of good luck. But in 1939, when I was in the second grade, the Japanese Army was defeated in the Nomonhan Incident and the military began to further expand its army and navy. My father was drafted for a second time and sent to northern China.

The Tripartite Pact was concluded in 1940. But this was followed by Japan's invasion of French Indochina in an attempt to control the prolonged unrest in China that followed the Second Sino-Japanese War. This aggravated US-Japan relations. The United States froze Japan's assets in their country and banned oil exports to Japan. Bilateral negotiations between the nations reached a deadlock, and Japan began preparing for war against the United States and Great Britain. During the summer of 1941, I was nine years old, and my father was drafted for yet a third time, less than two years after he had returned from northern China. He gave me a clear message before he left: "Since you are the first son, please protect our home, help your mother, and take care of your sisters and brothers." I remember the nervous feeling that something grave was happening. And indeed, in December of that same year, Japan plunged into World War II.

From the time of my parents' birth, Japan had been in seven wars including World War II. My childhood indeed appeared to be a product of war. In kindergarten, wooden guns were already in our classrooms. I was always fighting with someone and got a lump on my head many times. Since I was the first son under a patriarchal system, and on top of that, my father was not present, it seems that I acted big and quite violent to my mother and sisters even though in truth, I was sensitive.

I must have been a selfish, troublesome child. However, the presence of the nearby Takasaki station saved me around the time of my elementary school years. My house was about a 3-minute walk from the station, and I liked going there, standing on a nearby iron bridge, and getting covered by black smudge from steam engines passing beneath. I used to happily show off my face covered with soot. Inside the station, there was a timetable, which I started to memorize section by section. I knew the entire timetable before I knew the multiplication table in the second grade. My mother's ophthalmology clinic was adjacent to our house, and I would run into the waiting room and when I saw people looking at the timetable to check their next train, I would tell them, "the next train for Ueno will be at such and such," and I soon became the talk of my mother's patients. When I was in the third grade, I found a book titled, "National Train Timetable." I figured out from the timetable – and actually carried out the plan – that I could take the Takasaki Line bound for Tokyo, get off at the third station, called Jinbohara, where the train in the opposite direction would be waiting, and jump on that train to go back to Takasaki. I did this with only an entry ticket and went home as if nothing had happened. However, I never tried such a trip again as my mother immediately asked me where I had been.

Meanwhile, during the increasingly violent atmosphere and life at the time, my mother ordered books from

Shogakukan and Kodansha. My sister and I devoured picture books about people whom I had never heard of, such as Hideyo Noguchi, Lincoln, Edison, and so on, and I remember showing them to my classmates.

Then 1941 – the year that I remember most – came. My fourth-grade teacher was Mr. Mashimo, who was nicknamed "Rakkyo (white, pickled shallots)" since his forehead was bald. He was a music teacher. After making us all sit in front of the piano, he suddenly started playing music. Some started giggling as it was such an unconventional event, but I remember that my childhood self was moved by the piece because, for the first time in my life, it evoked serenity that seemed to speak to my heart. (I later learned that it was Schumann's Sonata.) I will never forget this incident since it made music my lifelong hobby. That summer, we found out that my father was in Taiwan, but he did not write about any details in his letter.

The most important experience of my life occurred in the summer of the fourth grade. During the long summer vacation, when I was cooling off in the evening in front of my house, I saw a few members of the neighborhood young men's association having a serious discussion over a map. It was about a mountaineering plan for five nights in Oze. I was driven by an urge to go with them and asked on the spot if they could take me too. They immediately dismissed my request as I was only nine years old, even though I was physically on the bigger side of boys my age. I insisted on going, and after I asked my mother to tell their mothers that I had been to an unexplored mountain with my father, the boys reluctantly agreed to take me with them. I learned from books that Oze consists of high mountains such as the famous Mt. Hiuchigadake and Mt. Shibutsu as well as Ozegahara, known for its wildflower fields and Ozenuma, the wetland. It touches the four prefectures of Gunma, Tochigi, Fukushima, and Niigata. Going there was a dream come true—as if I were on my way to an unknown country. When I put a 1.5kg bag of rice, rain gear, rice bowls, underwear, shoes and such in a backpack and tried to carry it, I fell backwards from the weight. But my mother and neighbors came to see me off. From Numata to Kamata, we rode a bus fueled by charcoal. As a matter of fact, there was no gasoline at the time, and for a fully loaded bus, just going up the Kuriu Pass was a challenge. People can now drive to the higher altitude and enjoy hiking in Oze, but that was not the case at the time. Moreover, we had to walk on a prefectural road for three hours from Kamata to Konaka, Tokura, and Oshimizu, to finally reach Sanpei Pass at the entrance of Oze.

We walked and walked in the glaring sun that summer. The backpack was biting into my shoulders and I could not stop sweating. My feet were hurting from blisters. Why did I ever come here? I wanted to wail but with so much sweating, I did not have any tears left. I endured as I did not want to bother others in the group.

We finally arrived at the gateway of Sanpei Pass, where the route turned into a steep uphill mountain path. Rocks were exposed and spring water was spouting here and there. Even a mouthful of the water was refreshing. One young man occasionally walked behind me and silently pushed my back, as I climbed with my jaw clenched. My feet were numb, and my head was empty. I breathed in fresh air whenever we stopped for a short break, and kept on going. Finally, we arrived at the top of the pass. The excitement of the moment when we reached the top is something I have never forgotten to this day, or rather, I cannot forget. In addition to a feeling of satisfaction that I had achieved something with my own strength, I still remember a sensation naturally welling up in me that could only be described as confidence, that even I could accomplish something if I made an effort. And I believe that this experience became the guidepost in the following years, for the course of my life. No one said anything to me, but I felt that the team members were relieved.

That night, we had dinner at the Chozo Hut, and I crashed without even changing my clothes. The following day we climbed Mt. Hiuchigadake with minimal gear. This time, my hurting feet felt lighter and we climbed at a slow pace for three hours. I was able to see mountains all around me. From the top of the four prefectures, we all relieved ourselves at the same time. We then enjoyed—from the bottom of our hearts—rice balls with sour plums and pickled radish we had prepared at the hut. After lunch, we spent time to fully enjoy the serene landscape of Ozenuma and Ozegahara. I still cannot forget the day when I spent time quietly looking at alpine plants such as Mizubasho (skunk cabbage). More than anything—there were not many people—the quiet and fresh air soothed my mind. We also climbed Mt. Shibutsu and descended from Hatomachi Pass as we observed snakes coiling and sleeping on the handrails of many bridges. By that time, I was a part of the team and as we went down the mountain, I sang along with everyone. I was proud of the great nature of my hometown that I had witnessed for the first time. When I returned home, I talked repeatedly about the entire experience to my mother, brothers and sisters. I was also proud of myself as the mothers of the neighborhood youths praised me.

On December 8th of the same year (December 7th in the US), Japan entered World War II. The war started with an attack on Pearl Harbor by the Japanese Navy, after which Japan landed on Malay, then the Philippines, and so on. We were all overjoyed with the news of victories and spent restless days in classes at school. My mother and I were always worried about my father. I was surprised to find pictures printed in the Jomo Newspaper of scenes at Lingayen Bay when he landed on Luzon Island, in the Philippines, in December around Christmastime. In January 1942, I received a short letter from my father saying that he had been moved to Manila and was staying safe. While we were worried about the uncertainty of the war, my father seemed to have been sent somewhere near Rabaul. According to what I learned later, at the time of the Fall of Singapore in 1942, part of the Japanese military had started discussing peace negotiations. Some expressed an opinion for promoting a compromise peace treaty at that time, and it seems that my father's superior was involved in that movement. However, as most of the military did not pay attention to such opinions, subordinates such as my father must have been demoted. I also found out later, that my father had landed on Guadalcanal Island around August, where he had bitter experiences for six months. He was lucky enough to survive and returned to Rabaul. All these are stories from my father.

Years later, in 1995, when I moved to the US and was working as the President of the Baltimore City Medical Society, the Maryland State Medical Society decided to compile war stories by US physicians and publish them in a special publication to celebrate the 50th anniversary of the ending of World War II. The Society requested me to write my childhood experience, that is, the perspective of Japan, in English. My childhood was formed during the war just like all other youths of my generation. However, I can never forget that many of those who were born before 1932, who were three or four years older than I am, became victims of the war.

Chapter Two

My Parents and Families

My father, Tasuku Nakazawa, was born in the Meiji era, the beginning of Japan's modern development. He was sent to battlefields as many as three times as a member of the Japanese Army. During the Battle of Guadalcanal until his miraculous return, he quite literally helped the country as his name ("tasukeru" or help) signifies; when at home, he joined the Imperial Rule Assistance Association (Taisei Yokusan Kai, 大政翼賛会). He also devoted himself to Takasaki City as a vice chairman after the war. However, now that I think back, probably because he survived a crisis in which he almost starved to death, it seems that he was never able to overcome his PTSD (as it is called now), and I have to say that his judgement became weaker due to psychological stress.

Although he was born as the 15th head of the Nakazawa family, the village headman, deep in the mountains of Sonohara, Tone County, Gunma Prefecture, he himself had to quit Numata Middle School after two years as the family's wealth had been declining over generations. He then joined the army as an aidman, was promoted to a lieutenant of the medical corps due to his effort, married my mother and had three sons and three daughters. What I noticed at the time of my childhood, though, was that my father was often away, and we boys, felt vulnerable without him to back us up in daily life. During this time, my mother often supported us on behalf of my father, in her own maternal style.

In spite of his frequent absences, I still remember my father as socially popular, tender-hearted, and generous. (In later years, out of his generosity, he became involved in his youngest brother's business in spite of risks. Due to this, our family hit rock bottom, financially.) My father's hobby was calligraphy–that is one thing we all remember about him without question. He went to China twice—particularly northern China— to visit regions associated with penmanship such as Taishan, and to purchase and send us a number of magnificent calligraphy items. It seems that he spent all his salary on such items. He used to tell us about outstanding calligraphy by Yan Zhenqing and Wang Xizhi, and I still cannot forget that he practiced writing until old newspapers became entirely black even when he was recovering from illness. In many ways, he fit the type of the eccentric military man.

My mother, Okimi Nakazawa, was unique in her own ways. A 1998 article titled, "Women's Social Advancement and the First Female Physician," from News No. 100, (celebrating the 100th anniversary of Takasaki municipality), describes her as follows:

> *"In 1928, Okimi Nakazawa opened her clinic as the first female doctor in Takasaki City. Okimi was born in Sagacho as the first daughter of Seijiro and Chii Ishida in 1904. She made up her mind to become a doctor as she nursed her sickly younger brother during her childhood. She graduated from Takasaki Women's High School and entered Tokyo Women's Medical Professional School (currently*

Tokyo Women's Medical University). She graduated in 1926 and interned at the Ophthalmology department of The University of Tokyo Hospital. She then returned to Takasaki and opened Ishida Ophthalmology Clinic in Yashimacho when she was 24 years old. In 1929, she married Tasuku Nakazawa, but the name of the clinic remained unchanged.

In Takasaki, ever since the Meiji era, many people suffered eye diseases such as trachoma, and my mother was extremely busy treating her patients every day. She was always kind and warm, and treated patients with a heart of benevolence. (As the saying goes, "medicine is a benevolent art.") She also listened to any consultation from her patients about bread-and-butter issues with openness and friendliness. Her motto was "love and peace, naturally and honestly," to which she was consistent throughout her life as a mother of three boys and three girls while balancing motherhood with her profession. After World War II, she established the "Takasaki Female Physicians' Organization" with her colleagues, and devoted herself in guiding and teaching younger generations as the first chairperson of the organization. [...] While the beginning of the Showa era was overshadowed by a dark recession, it was a fertile time for women's social and professional progress."

Among the stories that my mother always told us, the one I remember most was about Dr. Yayoi Yoshioka (1871-1959), who founded Tokyo Women's Medical School. As described in Japanese History of Female Doctors (1971), Dr. Yoshioka established Tokyo

Women's Medical School in 1900 and demonstrated the delivery of her own child to all her students as educational material. My mother admired "Yoshioka Sensei (Dr. Yoshioka)" and kept her "heart of devotion" to the end. Later when my mother was affected severely by my father's financial failure, she never showed her inner agony to her patients and managed to overcome the difficult time even though she was struggling every day to balance her family and her practice to make a living. She trusted and relied on me most, which now makes me feel undutiful to her for having traveled to and stayed in the United States. Though she visited me in the US over the years, spending a few months at a time, and becoming close to my children, in the end she always went back to Japan, saying that she was going home to my father.

My parents' posthumous Buddhist names are:

Yokusan In Taizan Gaho Kyoshi (翼賛院泰山雅峰居; Big brother who helped the Emperor and served his country for life, who loved the elegant peaks of Mt. Taishan)

Jigan In Shisei Chi-hi Ko Daishi (慈眼院至誠智悲光大姉; Big sister who cared for eyes with intelligent but saddened light)

My mother said to me in our last conversation: "I will go to Kamikochi with the members of my female doctors' organization. I will think of you who loved mountains. But I will never forgive you for leaving me." These were her last words to me. They still stick in my heart. That night, she had a wonderful time with her colleagues and then passed very suddenly. I feel relieved to know that she passed away without any suffering. To this day, I have never missed my morning and evening greetings and reporting on our family to her, and my wife and I offer homemade soup and cake before her photograph on her birthday and anniversary. I will never forget her support and encouragement during difficult times.

We six siblings have each lived our own unique lives. My sister, Sumiko, who is two years older than I am, was an excellent student and graduated from Tokyo Women's College. She worked as a teacher at a mission school, found a wonderful partner with whom she had two children, enjoyed their growing up, and then passed on. She used to call me "Bonchan" (which roughly means "daydreamer") and was always my guide. Since I was born close to the school cut-off date (which is April 1 in Japan), my sister was only one school year ahead of me and I was able to learn what she was doing at school. Thus, my sister probably thought that I was having an easy elementary school life without studying much. Both of her two sons became professors and are enjoying fulfilling and happy family lives.

My second sister, Setsuko, is two years younger than I am. She is a unique character who loves playing piano and was a swimmer who competed in the prefectural championships. She graduated from a music school in Tokyo and became quite busy as an instructor for her own piano school in Takasaki. I have heard that her only son has managed a number of excellent projects as an engineer.

My first younger brother, Kiyoshi, found his partner while he was studying law at Waseda University. He moved on to work for an oil company and successfully managed projects in the Middle East, mainly Kuwait. We visited him there in 1970, and I was impressed by his interest in the Middle East and its emergence, as well as by the fact that he was already forecasting the uprising of the Arab countries. As of 2019, he is living surrounded by his devoted wife, three daughters and their families.

My third sister, Toshiko, has always been interested in classical Japanese dancing. She told us that she wanted to become an accredited master instead of entering college, which she accomplished. She taught dancing until recently. She balanced her passion for dance with family life as a mother of one son and has been spending a calm and peaceful retirement.

Finally, my youngest brother, Takashi, was a "vagabond", which was also his nickname. As he aspired to become a sculptor, I invited him to Baltimore to attend and graduate from an art school. He spent some time in New York, went back to Japan and helped his wife, who is a bookbinder. They currently live in California. Their two daughters are married; one is in Japan and another is in the US

Our names, Sumiko (澄), Hiroshi (弘), Setsuko (節), Kiyoshi (清), and Toshiko (敏), are all related to Nakazawa (中澤), meaning "a flow of water." I believe that the last son's name, Takashi, carries my parents' wish for us to be prosperous. And in large part, we have all fulfilled that wish.

Chapter Three

World War II and Post-War Chaos

The Imperial Japanese Military opened the war at Pearl Harbor based on an assault strategy and won many battles in various other regions. I remember that when Japan took Singapore, we all danced with joy as the entire nation celebrated the victory. Takasaki Station became a bustling place with the shouting of "Banzai! Banzai!" as we sent soldiers off one after another. All of us fifth and sixth graders expressed our determination to attend the Military Academy or the Naval Academy in the future, and we praised and glorified militarism every day.

However, suddenly, on April 18, 1942, the Keihin (Tokyo-Yokohama) and Nagoya regions were air raided by bombers led by Lieutenant Colonel Doolittle of the United States. I remember everyone's shock at the news that our homeland had suffered damage for the first time. Two months later, the Battle of Midway occurred, and even though the Japanese Navy sustained devastating damage in which four aircraft carriers were destroyed, the Imperial Headquarters never told us these details but only reported successes in the south. Only the following year did I start to hear vague news about some kind of failure of the navy. And at the station, we started to receive more soldiers returning to the regiment as ash.

While we spent every day worrying about my father, whose whereabouts were unknown to us, the US Marines landed on Guadalcanal (August 6, 1942) and took over an airport that was being constructed by the Japanese Navy's landing forces and their construction workers. This was the first counterattack by the United States. It happened sooner than Japan had expected. And since the Japanese Military had lost the command of sea and air in the Battle of Midway, they could not deliver supplies to their troops on Guadalcanal. Now they were forced to retreat to the jungle due to US firepower on the ground. As a result, the Japanese military started to lose men to starvation, and many more were dying from malaria, amoebic dysentery, and malnutrition. These were the details my father corroborated years later, in relating his own narrow escape from death when he returned home from the war. Besides suffering severe hunger, my father had also been injured, and as an aidman but with no medicine, he had to crawl around the swampy jungle with his subordinates every night. With his eyes closed, my father would tell us how escaping from air raids and artillery fire that started early in the mornings was all he could manage in those days. I still remember his stories well.

In February of 1943, the Japanese Military had to retreat, and my father was sent somewhere near Rabaul by a navy destroyer. This was the first time the Japanese military shifted to defense since the opening of the war. My father repeatedly told us that the reason for Japan's defeat was firepower; there was a difference in national power. In Takasaki, we received many warnings by the military policemen not to say anything about what had happened at the front line. When I think of it now, I am amazed by how the Japanese military could send back injured soldiers to Japan at that time.

The war had started when I was in the fourth grade. My father was in Manila at the beginning of my fifth grade year. He landed on Guadalcanal in August of the same year, retreated to Rabaul in February 1943 where he recovered from his illness, and he was fortunate enough to board a ship bound for Japan via Palau in the north. That ship sank after being hit by a torpedo from a US submarine right on the equator, and my father was left floating in pitch-black oil with his subordinates for 14 hours before he was rescued by a Japanese destroyer, moved to a smaller ship, and after two weeks, finally arrived in Ujina Port. I still cannot forget when we received the telegram from Ujina. My mother was so happy that she was about to jump and hit the ceiling. And rightly so, since a few months prior to this good news, we had heard from a person in contact with my father's group that he was missing. My mother had been depressed from worrying about my father. Since he was stationed in Guadalcanal for six months, where only about 10,000 out of more than 20,000 soldiers had been able to retreat, the news that my father was coming home exhilarated us all beyond words, and it was literally the best of the best news.

But the soldiers who arrived in Tokyo Station all looked as if they were coming back from hell. They smelled horrible, their ribs were visible, they staggered even with canes, and their faces were blank. Some started crying, probably from the sense of relief to see their families in their hometown. My mother had gone to the station very early to wait for the train to arrive. But perhaps because she was nervous, she passed by my father at first, then backtracked in shock to see his condition. His weight seemed to be reduced by half, but he had not sustained any major injury. He managed to walk alone, but suffered from occasional malaria attacks of chills, and the conductor of his train had given him a layer of blankets. Other soldiers were in similar, or even worse condition than my father, but they made the trip by helping each other on the train. My mother brought my father's favorite food—although it was hard to get good food at the time—she made a Hinomaru Bento (white rice and a red pickled plum) and Kobumaki (rolled kelp with fish). My father enjoyed her food, promised everyone at the station to meet again and left for home. When he arrived at Takasaki Station, not only our family members but also his friends came to greet him. I had to help get my father home by putting his arm around my shoulder.

Although my father was a natural storyteller, he seemed to be quietly thinking about the ordeal even after his tension was relieved. Gradually, he started to reveal what had accumulated in his heart, but it was all about the United States. His first story was about the captured US doctors and aidmen whom my father met by coincidence. He told us that their medical practices were quite different from the German ones, which the doctors in the Japanese Military had learned, and he had a vague feeling that US methods were something new. Then he would frankly tell his family what he saw, saying that the United States was tough to defeat, and that their national power seemed to be on a level different from Japan's, judging from their firepower. A few times I immediately and emotionally objected to his opinion and went at him, saying, "the Japanese spirit will win in the end; we will place our flag at the White House for sure." However, in reality, even before my father had returned that summer, the Japanese Military on Attu Island was completely destroyed, and the United States landed on New Guinea. And as the second wave of retribution was carried out following Guadalcanal, we began to feel a little uneasy, even though we believed the final victory would come.

I became a sixth grader and dreamed even more about joining the Naval Academy to devote myself to the Japanese Navy and the country itself. In 1944, I took and passed the exam to enter Takasaki Middle School. I will never forget the day of the entrance ceremony. We took seats in the auditorium with our parents sitting in the back and listened to a speech by the principal. Since it was long and rather difficult to understand, I could see most of the students looking the other way and chatting, but I was intently listening to the speech. On the way home after the ceremony, my father told me, "Today's lecture by the principal was good. I was observing you from the back, and while all the other students were moving their heads or looking around, you did not even move, looking straight at the principal. You are able to focus. I was truly happy. Today really is a good day." It was the first time I had been praised by my father in 13 years. I had grown up not knowing my father at all, but now I felt I was finally able to communicate with him.

In spite of our patriotic hopes, the tide of the war was unfavorable to Japan. In June, we received news that the US military had landed on Saipan, where the Japanese garrisons were destroyed, and many women threw themselves from a cliff. In December, Japan lost Leyte Island, and the day I became a seventh grader, in 1945, the US military landed on Okinawa. Two months later, the Japanese military was no longer able to put up resistance and the attacks by B-29 bombers on the main island became intense. My father worked to give instruction for defense such as setting up air-raid shelters throughout Takasaki City.

The first- and second-year middle school students were not in the mood for studying; rather, we received thorough training under military instructors. I have a specific memory about this. I was a class captain, and when we were at a shoreside training at Lake Haruna, a petty officer of the navy made us all stand up straight and raise our arms, saying, "You lost the competition because you were all slacking!" and beat us on the buttocks with an oar. I was one who was beaten, but soon the only oar we had, broke in half and most of my classmates were spared. I still remember when they poked fun at me saying that, because I was sort of like a pioneer, I would always have to suffer. I was also called by other teachers to be beaten on the head while sitting on the floor so that I could not stand up straight right away, but staggered. More than half of my middle school era coincided with war and I did not master anything substantial. English was especially avoided as it was the enemy's language, and I truly regret how this affected my future. In particular, everyday English or English conversation was not taught until ten years after the end of the war.

In August, the atomic bombs were dropped on Hiroshima and Nagasaki. On August 15th, Japan agreed to unconditional surrender. But I remember my parents encouraged us at that time by saying, "Finally, from now, your generation begins."

Post-war Japan was chaos. We were a defeated nation for the first time in our history. Things were upside down, and more than anything, the cost of living, especially rice and daily necessities, skyrocketed due to unprecedented inflation. If you could pay, however, you could buy anything at the so-called black markets, which flourished both in cities and rural areas. We generally described the living standard as "i-shoku-ju (clothing, food, housing), but now it became "shoku-i-ju (food, clothing, housing) with food being the top priority. At our house, since six siblings had a great appetite, my mother increasingly complained that the food expenses were too high. At that time, we were a big family with our parents, our grandparents on my mother's side, and two nurses. Sometimes, my father and I would go to Niigata Prefecture by steam train to visit farmers and buy a small amount of rice at a high price, then come home late. Because it was black market, this was illegal, and police were stationed at each train stop to confiscate rice if someone was carrying more than 3.0kg. Some "professional rice porters" from Tokyo showed us their clothes, altered to have two layers so that they could fill the gap with rice. They claimed they could easily fit 7.5kg in these clothes. Our family managed to survive also with the help of my mother's patients from the countryside, who often shared their rice and vegetables.

In the fall of my second year at middle school, my father asked me if I could help him since he wanted to borrow a field from our neighbor to start farming. I, of course, replied, "let's do it!" but my school life was becoming busier. I was again the class captain and felt quite uneasy, but my brothers and sisters were still young, and no one but I would be able to help my father.

I made a plan to come home early from school, not join any circles such as sports clubs, and do homework after the farm work. In this way, my father and I started seriously imitating farmers. The borrowed land was far away, about an hour and half on foot from our house, which could be more than 30 minutes even by bike. As a result, I only had half a day on Saturdays and a full day on Sundays to work on the farm. I knew that it was an impossible task but had no other choice because we needed to have food for our family.

One difficulty was pulling the heavy cart full of fertilizer—human feces of course. Every house had a full septic tank at the time, so everyone in the neighborhood was happy when my father and I picked up their waste. Whenever I went around the houses and gave courtesies to them, I heard them say in shock, "Is this the noble son of the Nakazawa family?" but I did not pay attention to it as I put my heart into my task. My father and I carried full buckets and placed them on the cart; my father would get on the bike, and I would push the cart surrounded by the stench.

This was our routine. I tilled the field, sowed seeds, watered the land, applied the fertilizer, and removed weeds. During winter, I trod out the wheat in the middle of freezing "dry winds" unique to our region while managing to repeat English words that I had learned over the week. In spring, we started with the preparation for rice planting, drew water to our 0.5-acre field, and with the help of a few others, planted rice seedlings given to us by other farmers. This was how we took our first steps to produce rice. During my summer vacation, I spent my time weeding and fertilizing. When I came home, I would go for a swim in the municipal pool, then come home and read some books for school at night.

Around that time, chemical fertilizers started to go around, and some farmers applied them to their rice fields. The growth of their seedlings was outstanding, and I was surprised to see the blue-green color of the plants were different from our feces-nourished seedlings. Later, I learned that their harvests were exceptional. While we harvested 330kg of rice, those who used chemicals harvested 390kg or more. Their outcome was completely beyond ours. After our harvest, we had to give 120kg of rice to the landlord, but the rest was ours. In fall, after harvesting and threshing the rice, we had our first "white rice" made by ourselves for dinner. We all put our hands together and gave our prayers of gratitude.

My father taught us that the Chinese character for rice (米) represents the 88 (八十八) tasks involved in rice cultivation so that we could finally taste it. He emphasized that we should never forget to keep making an effort in all areas. My mother went to share the rice, along with other vegetables from the field such as daikon radishes, sweet potatoes and green onions, with our neighbors who had helped us, saying, "Hiroshi made this rice." Thanks to the harvest, we did not have to go to the black market for food for a while.

This life of working in the field continued from the second to fourth years of my middle school. However, I felt that I had not done enough studying to continue my education. At school, as I heard about the exams for high school, I gradually started to feel impatient. I asked my father for permission to quit the farm work. My father agreed, and decided to return the field to the landlord, as the work was too much for one person.

Chapter Four

Decision to Become a Physician and Relocation to Tokyo

Back then, I had made up my mind to become a physician and carry out the family business; however, my academic status and my progress in preparing for the entrance exam were not very promising. There was a class offered after dinner that allowed our grade to participate in a special course for 10th graders. The lecture was specifically catered to preparation for the entrance exams, and I felt overwhelmed.

My first choice was to attend public institutions, such as Urawa High School and to attend Gunma University to study medicine, as both were located in geographically convenient areas from home. Some people suggested that I participate in exams for multiple private institutions in order to get familiar with the setting. So I went to the entrance exam for Seijo High School (of the old education system) located in Setagaya-Ku, Tokyo.

I can clearly remember when I visited the campus for the first time. There was a long street leading to the school with gingko trees lining both sides of the road. The campus was buried in the greenery of Musashino, which cultivated a somewhat relaxed atmosphere that made me feel great. I thought I had managed to survive the exam, in contrast to my personal interview. In the interview, I had been very nervous when they asked me about athletic activities. I had nothing to show except that I had enjoyed sumo wrestling since elementary school, which led me to wrestle a bit.

Two weeks later, I was excited by an acceptance notice, but I was hesitant to ask my parents for enrollment there, because the high tuition at the private institution would burden them. Their supportive response freed me from my concern, as they told me to make my own decision. Immediately, I decided to choose Seijo High School over Urawa High School. Seijo High School was said to be "preppy," and most of the students were the relaxed offspring of well-to-do families.

As I found out later, the majority of them were from the upper-middle class and had continued to Seijo High School from the elementary school. But they were not at all just "relaxed" kids; they were smart and had good business sense, and I was very impressed by quite a few of them. My older readers might remember the way high school students in the old-system wore their ragged school uniforms everywhere while marching and singing dormitory anthems on the street. I have clear memories of my pride in being among those who stayed in a dormitory, with the opportunity to be academically mentored by upper classmen with philosophical cannons, such as Kant, Hegel, and Nishida.

Soon, there were challenges in the shift from the old to new schooling systems. My class had lasted only one year in the old education system. The new system placed us in a high school and moved us to college during the year that followed. Also, our newly acquired knowledge of German suddenly became irrelevant in the new system. Most of my classmates were aiming to get into Tokyo University at the Komaba campus. I also learned that anyone who aspired to be in medicine was required to take a separate entrance exam for the Department of Medicine after two years of general study.

Considering the six years of tuition required to obtain a degree in medicine, private universities were out of my scope. I had to get into a public institution. I worried that I was not yet ready for acceptance to Tokyo University. As I had feared, a year later, in 1949, I failed the entrance exam. I cried out of disappointment. But my older sister consoled me. I have never forgotten the way she said "Bon-chan, you are still young. As people say, life is full of ups and downs, this is nothing but a milestone for you." She patted my shoulder.

Everything might have been going too well for me. Now I convinced myself that I should be humble and go back to where I had started. That one year at Seijo High School had given me the type of lessons that have resonated throughout my life ever since. The founder of Seijo High School, Dr. Masataro Sawayanagi was from Nagano prefecture, and his vision of true education was to learn in the midst of a natural environment. He had founded Seijo High School to help students develop their individuality. (In 2018, this institution celebrated 100 years of existence.) Dr. Sawayanagi promoted three imperatives of education: 1) respect for originality, 2) development of self-reliance and self-confidence, and 3) constant striving for ultimate truth. He encouraged us to be the very best that we could be. Back then, most of the students exhibited outstanding and unique characteristics; however, I overlooked the other two imperatives. It wasn't until years later that I understood them. Considering my upbringing in the countryside, Seijo High School taught me many things.

In Tokyo, aside from academic study, I was able to experience live music and opera for the first time. I had opportunities to meet with famous writers and painters and hear their stories in person. That one year was like a springboard to many aspects of my later life. While my parents worked hard to send me money, I was busy following my curiosity and experiencing what life had to offer.

After student life in Seijo High School, I started studying for the entrance exam in the coming year. Luckily, a dormitory run by the Housing Committee of the Association of Gunma Residents allowed me to stay there, and I lived among people from Gunma prefecture. I did not sign up for prep courses but rather studied on my own by reviewing textbooks and study magazines.

During that time, my father had gotten involved in business with his brother. I started noticing that my father was economically struggling after multiple operational mistakes. In the meantime, I made a solid decision to become a physician. I also realized that I might have a better chance being accepted into Chiba University than Tokyo. Contrary to the previous year that had brought such joy and richness into my life, 1949 brought days that were quite difficult for me.

In March of 1950, I was accepted into the program of my first choice, the School of Arts and Sciences at Chiba University. My entire family told me that they felt very happy for the first time in many years. But after two years of study, another entrance exam would be waiting for me. I looked for tutoring jobs near my dormitory and taught mathematics to a few high school students in order to cover some daily expenses. As it took two hours to get to Chiba, both my time and money were quickly expended. While the tuition was not as high as the private school had been, I still tried to live thriftily to reduce the stress on my parents. There was no way I could date a girl. My free time was scattered throughout my days like bits and pieces, so I put in as much effort to study as much as I could.

Two years flew by, and 1952 seemed to come abruptly. Without having been able to celebrate the New Year, the day of the exam, March 1st, arrived. The application ratio was approximately 1 to 3.2. My competitors had completed all required college courses and studied for two to three years. I was hoping not to travel from Tokyo, but to stay in Chiba on the day of the exam for my mental and intellectual well-being.

It was a great relief when one of my classmates from Seijo High School, who lived 15 minutes away from the Department of Medicine, offered to let me stay in his home, telling me that his parents would welcome me. He was applying for the Engineering program and said that there was no need to worry about him. I appreciated him from the bottom of my heart and happily accepted the offer and stayed there.

We did not foresee what happened the next morning. Snow had started on the night before the first day of the exam. When I arrived at the exam site, I heard that applicants from Tokyo were arriving late due to a delay in the train schedule. I worried about one of my best friends from the School of Arts and Sciences who lived in Ryogoku, Tokyo.

In spite of the inclement weather, the proctor commanded in a short sentence, "It's time for us to start now," and in fact, the exam papers had already been distributed. I worried so much about the whereabouts of my friend that I had difficulty focusing on the math section of the exam. I needed to make an effort to bring my mind back to the exam.

After about a half hour, a few dozen applicants had come running in to the test site. I felt awful as I glanced at my best friend's face. He was red and appeared to be angry. However, I was focusing on a math problem at that moment, so my concern quickly faded out. I did not say anything to him after the exam other than the fact that I saw him.

But in spite of the extra difficulty for him on the exam day, he was accepted into the Department of Medicine a year later. In fact, he had done so well that he eventually obtained a position as a professor in pediatric surgery at Chiba University and in later years, was recognized as a laureate.

Luckily, I was also able to get into the medical school. On the morning the results were announced, the mother of one of my friends who was accepted at Tokyo Medical and Dental University, called me from

Takasaki with the good news saying, "Congratulations Hiroshi-san. You got accepted to the Department of Medicine at Chiba University."

Back then, my mother was under a lot of stress due to the failing business my father had gotten involved in. When I shared my good news with her, she broke out into a full smile just like the time when she jumped up upon receiving a telegram that read, "Return soon," reporting my father's return from the war. Now she held me close and cried, "That's great. That's great." She did not let me go for a long time.

My friend from Seijo High School who lived in Chiba also called to congratulate me and said that he had gone to Chiba University to confirm my acceptance. I was able to speak with his parents and show my appreciation to them for taking me in, explaining how lucky I was to be able to stay overnight at their house. I was deeply appreciative of the luck that Seijo High School had brought to me.

Chapter Five

My Parents' Financial Struggles and My Early Independence at Medical School

Contrary to the fortunate situation on my end, my father continued struggling with his business. My mother's depression was getting worse by the day, and she started closing her clinic from time to time because she had difficulty taking in patients. A psychologist worked with my mother, but her progress was not easy. There were even times when her condition was bad enough to threaten my siblings' hope for their futures. My older sister worked as a school teacher and supported my mother, but my father was taking too much of the money to pay off his debts, and I was helpless to change the situation from afar.

While my classmates had started the medical school year under celebratory cherry blossoms, progressing toward their medical degrees, my heart was torn to pieces. As I look back, I realize that I must have had extraordinary confidence to have kept my head above water. I had relocated to a housing facility in Narashino. My daily commute to the main campus in Chiba was two hours. All the boarding students were from outside of the Tokyo-Chiba area, ranging from freshmen to senior students. The student housing was a quiet but insightful atmosphere for me.

In my college, freshmen were required to sign up for anatomical science. The lab work involved autopsies that demanded much effort. My career aspiration was to become a surgeon, so I was motivated to obtain a solid foundation in basic anatomical knowledge and our collaborative work often continued until late into the night. Dr. Morita at Chiba University was famous in the field of anatomical science. He had studied in Germany, and the majority of his lecture was offered in German. I felt at home in his course because I had studied German during my year at Seijo High School.

The final class exam consisted of identifying body tissue. In the exam, we were asked to randomly pull out one prepared slide from a jar for microscopic observation. This exam was a major hurdle. If we failed, the professor would say "wiederkommen" (retry) and schedule us to take a makeup exam one month later. Approximately half of our class experienced this fate. But when the professor asked me to identify my tissue sample, I confidently responded that my slide was part of the brain, specifically an oligodendroglia cell. I will never forget the big smile he gave at my answer, as I passed the exam.

To cover some of my daily expenses, I tutored mathematics on Saturdays and Sundays, to nearby high school students. Luckily, I had been granted tuition remission. Tuition was 3,600 yen per year and at that time, 1 US dollar was worth 360 yen, so tuition was 10 dollars per year. The tuition for a medical student at a private institution was ten times more than that of public institutions.

During the two-month summer recess, a relative in Ichikawa allowed me to stay there and I was able to save up some money by working as a salesperson for ice-cooling refrigerators at Tokyo-Nihonbashi Mitsukoshi Department Store. Although at that time, I had no experience in sales, I tried my best to explain the products and their functions to customers. My efforts not only led to customers being satisfied but also to my supervisor being satisfied. I was able to spend some money for my siblings when I returned home at the end of August.

Due to my adventures in earning money outside of school, I often missed classes. Although I needed the money for my daily expenses, I would not recommend that anyone else do this. One day in late spring, I was on a train looking out of a window on the green rice fields of Narashino. The scenery took me back to my green rice field during the second and third years of my middle school.

Suddenly a thought struck my mind—parasites often plagued children, especially ascaris. Of course, I myself had handled human waste as fertilizer, thus parasites, too, but what is the ascaris situation among elementary school children in this area? My intellectual curiosity now grew insatiable, and the next day I left the University early to visit a school doctor in an elementary school near the railroad line. I explained that I was a medical student interested in conducting fecal examinations among elementary school children and offered to provide the school with my study's results. The doctor told me that she would consult with the school principal and get back to me. I had moved one step forward in my research.

When I returned to my dorm, I found four students who were willing to collaborate with me. We decided to charge some fees for our testing, so I contacted the school doctor and suggested that each fecal examination would cost 5 yen. One month later, she obtained permission from the PTA to spend the money, and the study was approved.

We went to the school and picked up a big box full of matchboxes containing fecal samples. In a small empty room in our dorm, we used three sets of university-owned microscopes, one lamp, a basin filled with cresol, and most importantly, an image of Ascaris on the side. At last, we were ready to start microscopic examinations. To our surprise, we found positive results in one case after another. The prevalence of ascaris was nearly 90% along with a few cases of hookworm. When I brought the results back to the elementary school, the doctor was also surprised at the high rate.

I started to wonder what could be causing the high prevalence of cases, as most of the farmers in the area used pesticides that were thought to kill parasites. So, I started a study group in my dorm. The elementary school contacted me to ask for my assistance in planning an intervention to prevent the continued spread of the problem because the PTA was highly concerned about the prevalence of cases.

One of the alumni who owned a private clinic suggested that I speak with some pharmaceutical companies and request samples from them, so I followed his advice. Upon receiving a set of medications, we planned for the school doctor to prescribe those medications to the elementary school students and to conduct another 5-yen exam two weeks from the intake date.

What helped us was the pharmaceutical companies being so cooperative. This was because there were not many large-scale studies focused on fecal examinations of elementary school children that provided a viable random sampling. After two weeks of medication, the results of the retest found that the prevalence rate was less than 50%. The medication was proven to be somewhat effective, and the school officials were very happy with our study.

The school doctor was one of the alumni of Chiba University, as he had graduated from Chiba Medical College under the old education system; therefore, I had disclosed the fact that all study members were struggling medical students. We were all making an effort to reduce the financial burden on our parents. After this study, there were additional requests from a few elementary schools to repeat our investigation, so we were able to save some money toward our futures.

At the end of the first school year, I was very happy to obtain an A in anatomical science and the bare minimum grades for other subjects, which would allow me to continue as a sophomore. The focus during my second year of study was pathological science. While we learned the pathological elements of a healthy body during the first year, the second year allowed us to study valuable information about the ways our bodies react when we are ill, as well as how to investigate the root cause of clinical symptoms.

I asked some freshmen to continue the fecal examinations as I gradually shifted my focus toward clinical work. Luckily, Dr. Fukuda of Labor Physiology was an alumnus of Seijo High School. He was interested in issues of blood pressure and had conducted a study in Akita prefecture focusing on the correlation between salt intake and blood pressure. I was able to be a part of his research team. It did not provide a stipend, but it provided meals, and opened up a space for me to learn.

Back then, trains to areas in the Tohoku region like Akita typically departed from Ueno Station around 10:00 in the evening. I had to wait in a long queue with other medical residents to get on the train. It was at full capacity with no seats available, so I spread a newspaper out and lay down by putting my upper body under a seat while my lower body was left out in the aisle. Other medical residents were in the same condition, trying to catch a good night's sleep and prepare for the next day's work.

I was able to fall soundly asleep; however, the staff had to wake me up when the train stopped at a station. We ran to a 1-minute noodle stand located on the platform, ordered, ate quickly then jumped back on the train. I remember that we repeated this trick at one station, but I cannot recall the name of the station if it was "Kohriyama." Now this practice may be considered strange, but at the time it was a typical long-distance travel practice.

Medical residents were doctors who typically worked in the field of general medicine and worked to obtain a PhD in Medicine a few years before starting their own private practices. Back then, the title of "Doctor in Medicine" carried such value! But once, I found out that there had been a medical doctor whose doctoral degree research had been "a study on the testicles of fleas" before he opened up a private practice as a surgeon. As such information was usually not shared with patients, doctors must have been able to earn the trust of patients solely with their credentials.

I was determined to learn as much about human medicine as I could. Now I was working in a farming village with a high prevalence of high blood pressure. I enjoyed meeting with many residents in the village to measure their blood pressure and record the data. As Akita is famous for rice, I was happy to stuff my stomach with delicious rice and pickles. And though I cannot drink and am therefore unable to speak of them much, the regional specialty sakes named "Ranman" and "Taiheizan" were provided nightly, and the village residents surprised me with their hospitality. When I visited the Tohoku region for the first time, I was especially moved by the humility of the people there. And the return ticket allowed me to travel along the coast of the Sea of Japan, whose vicious waves and magnificent sunsets remain a vivid memory of mine.

During that year—1953—an unforgettable event happened. News confirmed the success of a British Mt. Everest expedition. Sir Edmund Hillary's words: "the secret to success is to start. The rest is to continue moving toward the goal," were an empowering message to me. I appreciate his quote as it motivated me when I struggled in later years. Considering that the expedition of Naoki Uemura of Japan succeeded 17 years later, the level of teamwork between the expeditioners must have been splendid.

Since my sophomore year was preoccupied with tutoring jobs, my academic work was secondary to me. But I had managed to obtain an A in pathology and was somewhat satisfied with the school year.

During my junior year, I registered for clinical courses but became overwhelmed. I totally removed myself from the fecal examination project, but the lower classmen happily carried out what was left of it. When I started to worry about ways of earning my daily expenses, my maternal uncle helped me obtain a summer job. He had studied liberal arts at Hirosaki High School and later studied law at Tokyo University. After his graduation, he was ordered to enlist, and World War II had ended when he was in North Korea, so he was incarcerated in Siberia for 7 years. Luckily, he returned home alive in the end.

This uncle had introduced me to one of his classmates from Hirosaki High School who had graduated from Chiba Medical College and opened a private practice in Choshi city. Dr. Katakura, then, offered me a summer position on the condition of staying with him in Choshi and assisting in his daily work while learning surgical medicine hands-on. I was very happy. My stay in Choshi was for two months total, and each day I learned practical aspects of clinical practice as Dr. Katakura's second assistant. At night, I reviewed all the surgeries that took place during the day and studied the operations scheduled for the following day. Every day, I appreciated the generosity of Dr. Katakura and his family.

When the clinic was closed on Sundays, I took a walk to Inuboezaki and enjoyed the landscape where the Tone River met the Pacific Ocean, as well as the white-colored vessels that cruised afar toward the north. One day, a fisherman told me, "They're heading to America, young man." At that moment, I was struck by the thought of visiting another country for the first time in my life. My father had been born in an area upstream of the Tone River, I was born mid-stream, and there I was standing at the mouth of the river looking at the white vessels on the horizon—I felt as if that moment connected me with my destiny.

At the end of August, I thanked Dr. Katakura and his family, as I was able to bring numerous staple foods from Chiba as souvenirs, such as dried seafood and peanuts. But back home, it was disheartening for me to see my father suffering with chronic high blood pressure and depression from his work, and my mother barely operating her clinic just to stay above water.

Back at the university that fall, I wanted to relieve my feelings of stagnation, so I decided to join a theater club where I could perform on stage and learn to have confidence in front of an audience. Critics were gentle toward me. At the University Clinic, instructors occasionally told me, "I haven't seen you around here before," which made me sweat out of nervousness. I received an invitation from Dr. Fukuda to join his research project in Akita, but I was concerned about the balance between earning an income and practicing medicine.

Based on the information I had gathered at the dorm, medical graduates signed up for internships that were typically non-paid with just a few exceptions for positions in rural areas. After completion of the internship, people started working in an unpaid medical residency at an institution for three to four years. It wasn't until around the fifth year when people usually began to receive a salary as a medical assistant.

Of course, often people worked in the rural areas to earn income prior to starting work in a medical residency. Originally, I had wanted to work at Tokyo Daiichi Hospital (Center Hospital of the National Center for Global Health and Medicine). However, it was impossible for me to go there without monetary support for housing and other daily expenses, so I quickly abandoned it as an option.

When I started hearing from others in the dorm, I found out that an upperclassman was accepted for an intern position at the United States Naval Hospital in Yokosuka. He related every small detail to me. Listening to him, my excitement soared so high that my head seemed to pound like an earthquake. I had difficulty falling asleep that night. I soon came to learn, however, that all the exams for this internship required reading, writing, and oral English skills. Though I had attempted to listen to a radio program called "Come, Come, everybody!" on a few occasions, I had very little English conversation skill, and my written exams in English had never exceeded 30 points out of 100. My

German conversation skills were of no use, and I did not know what to do as my junior year was almost over.

At the beginning of my senior year, I coincidentally found a script from an American movie. It was from a small booklet that consisted of scripts written in English on one side and Japanese on the other. I had tried to find ways to learn English conversation from native speakers in the past, at churches in Chiba and also in Tokyo. However, there was no US military base in Chiba, and I started to worry, as I needed to use my limited time to learn English with as much efficiency as possible. So, here it was—I purchased the booklet. I desperately memorized the entire script of the movie by mumbling every single line over again as I waited for the opening day of the movie. Of course, I needed to travel to Tokyo to see the movie. I arrived at the theater in the morning, ate tangerines and bread with sweet bean paste for lunch, and recited the lines I had learned during the intermission. During the second viewing, I was focused on the tone and the movement of mouths. I was only half awake during the night viewing, and I was asleep on the train out of Chiba at ten that evening.

For a while, I followed this crazy weekend schedule for each new movie. I would review the script and spend all day on Sundays watching the movie while trying to master English conversation. All I can remember now are the faces of James Dean and Cary Grant. It was funny how this practice would turn out to save me later.

At that time, Dr. Komei Nakayama, an alumna of Chiba University, was very famous. He was recognized as a young leading esophageal surgeon and was popular among students. He offered much encouragement to students and shared stories during his lectures after he returned from his professional trips to the United States.

One day, I could not help but speak with him in regard to my personal concerns and my future. He told me, "The United States might be one option for you. You could visit there for a few years and come back to Japan for medical residency. Or, you could stay there longer and do some substantial work before you come back. Either way, it requires a firm decision."

As just one of his students among many, I was happy to receive this much of his attention, and his advice exceeded my expectations. Dr. Nakayama agreed to write me a recommendation letter for the intern position at the US Naval Hospital in Yokosuka. He did so for the sake of my future, but as I was just one of his many students, I felt exceedingly honored to receive his recommendation.

The final semester of my final year was approaching. My first exam was for the intern position and it was followed by the national exam scheduled for eighteen months later. As only a few of my classmates and I had gone to the exam for the US Naval Hospital in Yokosuka, we were surprised to see 58 individuals in the waiting room for the test for a program that was hiring only four interns each year.

I spoke with other applicants and found that the majority of them were in the same position I was in. This hospital, along with the Army Hospital and Air Force Hospital, offered room and board, and provided a salary that amounted to thirty dollars (1,8000 yen), so it was a dream job. The position also offered the opportunity to work in the United States in the future. Simply put, it was the ultimate training program in the nation.

I was able to clear nearly half of the written exam, but I was uncertain of my results. In the afternoon, I took the oral exam. My examiner was a six-foot-five Naval Lieutenant with a rugged, extremely serious air about him. I was nervous. The first question was about heart attacks. My response lasted approximately one minute, as I could not give too many details. The next question was on appendicitis. I was wondering if I was answering his questions correctly, so I responded slowly while observing his reaction.

Then, he asked me where I had learned English. I responded with "Actually, through movies. I learned English through American films." Suddenly, he stood up with the loudest and heartiest laugh I had ever heard. I was soaked with sweat from nervousness, but he continued, "I noticed a bit of a Southern accent. Was your teacher James Dean?" I answered "Yes, indeed he was." I did not know anything about Southern accents.

I thought I might have failed the exam, so I looked at the clock. I still had 15 minutes. I felt better answering the next question. He asked me to talk about my family, so I started telling him about my parents. He did not ask me about my father; however, when I told him my mother was an ophthalmologist, he leaned in for the first time. As he had never heard about female doctors in Japan, he started asking me various questions. My mother was the first female doctor in the region, and she struggled with raising six offspring during and after the war—I was very surprised at my ability to speak of her in fluent English (with a Southern accent).

He then, shared with me that he was from a mountain town in Pennsylvania, and continued struggling even after he had relocated to Baltimore City. He had graduated from the University of Maryland with a medical degree, completing his internship and residency prior to enlistment in the navy. He had four children and one on the way.

I told him about earning some money by conducting fecal examinations, which had allowed me to graduate. I felt that I earned some points there.

At four in the afternoon, all the applicants were gathered for the announcement of the results—those who passed the exam were announced. The first place went to Katsumi Miyai from Keio University, the second went to Yasuo Yamauchi from Tokyo University, the third went, surprisingly, to me, and the fourth to Sadao Morikawa from Kobe University. I was excited and speechless, as those of us who had passed congratulated each other. I felt sad when I saw the disappointed faces of those who did not pass. When I thought of how cruel life could really be at times, I felt empathetic toward them.

Back at home, my parents were happy to see my plan for the near future resolving itself. Their financial situation was deteriorating further, and I felt a wave of guilt for noticing, as I felt as though I was the only one in the family who continued to stay afloat.

At last, my graduation was near. One week before the ceremony, I was asked unexpectedly to come to the Student Service Office, where the chair of the office told me that at the previous class meeting, there was a unanimous decision selecting me to present the student commencement address at the graduation ceremony. It was a collective request of me from every one of my classmen. But it had been decided without my vote, and I immediately responded that it would be more appropriate for the Summa Cum Laude to give the speech.

But when the chair put his head down as though he was imploring me to present the address, I had no choice but to accept the decision. I managed to deliver the address smoothly at the ceremony, and it brought back memories of the times in which I had struggled. I truly felt that my graduation would not have been possible without the generosity and support of many people, and the speech allowed me to express my sincere appreciation to the professors and family members who had aided me.

Chapter Six

The United States Naval Hospital Yokosuka: The Beginning of My New Life

The US Naval Hospital, Yokosuka, was a large-scale hospital that had 300 in-patients, and the hospital was running at full capacity when I started working there. Although two years had passed since the Korean War, the hospital received an influx of soldiers with injuries, complications such as inflammation, and trauma that required emergency care. As most of the patients arrived in the evening and throughout the night, we struggled for the first few months.

Our job was to work amongst medics coordinating triage for the ER, to conduct preliminary exams on in-coming patients, to initiate diagnostics under the instruction of the Chief Medical Officer, and to provide treatment by supporting the American nurses. This position allowed me to experience situations that I never had before. In the beginning, I had an extremely difficult time because everything was communicated in English. It was especially difficult when most of the patients, who were soldiers, were experiencing such agonizing pain and other adverse symptoms, that they were unable to communicate clearly even in English. I could not help but feel as if I was walking on eggshells, and felt I always needed others' assistance in order not to miss major symptoms and significant details in a patient's medical history.

It seemed like every night I was on assignment at the Obstetrics department, pregnant women (American wives) in labor would arrive as soon as I had fallen asleep. Nearly 90% of the emergency visits happened around three or four o'clock in the morning when we were in the deepest sleep. In the mornings that followed, by 7:30 am, interns were required to be ready at an operating room if assigned to the surgical unit or to conduct a preliminary examination before a physician arrived if assigned to the internal medicine unit, in order to receive questions from doctors.

In those days, shame or pride were the least of my concerns—I was simply trying to get by day after day fully utilizing my body and mind. I was totally at a loss for the first two months, but after that everything slowly started to come together for me. I remember feeling very much relieved about how lucky I had been to survive without making any big mistakes.

In the surgical unit, the chief thoracic surgeon, Dr. Frye of the University of Michigan, happened to be a great friend of Dr. Nakayama and was very nice to me. My hands-on training at Katakura Clinic also came in handy. I became interested in surgical methodology, especially American techniques. Although I was not able to pinpoint the detailed distinctions between Japanese and American methodologies, I noticed some fundamental differences.

Every three months, we rotated units, but we still had some fun between the heavy workloads. At the top of my fun list was the dining hall. Since interns were ranked as commissioned officers, we were allowed to dine at the officers' mess hall or at a dining room that served high quality American cuisine for each meal. The generous and unlimited servings of beef were especially memorable to me because it was the thickest and the most flavorful beef that I had ever tasted. The grilled salmon and other seafood are also worth mentioning.

During the night shift, at two in the morning, we were able to eat huge steaks in the naval diner amongst the sailors. From time to time, I got so full that I was too uncomfortable to fall asleep. My favorite party event was the bimonthly gathering where I ate roast piglets with officers and their families. Those gatherings offered relaxing time for us to sit down and talk, or to sing along to a piano, which gave me the opportunity to learn a couple of American songs.

But much as I loved the American food, I appreciated that Dr. Mohri in Yokosuka City ordered Japanese dishes, which not only satisfied our tastes but also nourished our weary psyches, dissipated after so many days filled with nothing but American culture.

My examiner, Dr. Henry Holljes taught internal medicine, with a focus on inflammation and communicative diseases. Because of my experience with him at the entrance exam, I felt a strong connection with him. However, I could not have then imagined what a significant role he would play in determining my future by later arranging for me to study in the United States.

Four of us interns were divided into two groups, and we took turns covering night shifts every-other day. During my time off, I often visited an antenatal clinic operated by Doctors Takaaki and Chie Mohri. They had worked in one of the clinics that were designated to perform abortions under the Eugenic Protection Act, for Japanese women who had gotten pregnant by American soldiers.

They had invented a hysteroscope to examine the movement of the fetus, and I was given a chance to observe a fetus in the uterus before an abortion was to take place. Since the Eugenic Protection Act was a unique circumstance of the post-war era, this sort of image was only observable during that short period, and an opportunity I appreciated.

At the end of the year, when we became qualified to study in the United States, we started the application process for some US university hospitals and started submitting application forms along with recommendations from our alma maters. Four of us chose institutions in the Midwestern states—Yamauchi chose the University of Michigan, Miyai chose Washington University in St. Louis, Morikawa sought a residency position at the University of Wisconsin. I wanted to study under Dr. O.H. Wangensteen at the University of Minnesota, however, my position went to an American student instead, possibly due to some administrative matter.

I received this news in February. We were scheduled to be released from the hospital in Yokosuka in March. I panicked and wrote a letter to Dr. Holljes who had returned to Baltimore and opened a private clinic three months prior. He was my last resort to study in the United States, as it was already too late to apply for a position in other institutions. His response brought me unexpected joy.

It read "Hospitals in the United States all offer an annual contract. They may allow you to stay or may ask you to go elsewhere after one year. With your current level of English, you may have experienced much difficulty even if you were to be accepted into the University of Minnesota. Residency in the surgical unit is likely to have many applicants and will therefore be extremely competitive. In environments where American physicians complete their residency, your chances for success are extremely scarce. I am Catholic, so I worked as an intern for one year at Saint Agnes Hospital in a suburb of Baltimore after I graduated from the University of Maryland. I then applied for a residency position in the Department of Internal Medicine at Johns Hopkins University. I believe that Saint Agnes Hospital is the best option for you, and I would like to suggest that you complete an internship there. If you would like to do so, I can coordinate with the hospital to secure your position. Please let me know your opinion."

It was such a wonderful piece of news to me, and I responded by agreeing to his recommendation offer. Although the school year in the United States starts in September, the fiscal year of hospitals starts July 1st. That meant I needed to be in the United States no later than June. But I could not enter the country without a visa which required evidence of employment in the United States. Within two weeks, I had received a letter offering me an internship at Saint Agnes Hospital.

Through that commotion, my parents seemed to have mixed feeling about my decision. My father was bedridden after a stroke. My mother was anxious about losing me to the United States, which I completely understood. But I felt that everything was the best it could have been, considering that the US Naval Hospital was doing so much to assist a poor struggling student like myself. And on top of it all, Dr. Holljes was helping me study abroad. To keep up my spirits, I would listen over and over to Beethoven's Symphony No.5 in C Minor, as the drums in the opening resonated with my mood and inspired me.

My next problem was the travel cost. The exchange rate was one US dollar to 360 yen. A one-way flight cost 300 dollars, which was 100,000 yen. The Fulbright Transportation Scholarship had offered a grant program for scholars with secured education funding and/or employment in the United States which would pay for a roundtrip ticket upon passing the exam. All four of us jumped at this opportunity; however, unfortunately, I ended up being the only one who failed.

With his generosity, Dr. Holljes had found me a job; however, I could not get there. I could not even ask my parents, as they had debt. I was deeply disappointed; then a couple of young American navy doctors made me an offer, saying "We will figure it out and pay for you to get there. You can pay us back once you start working." I could not believe what had happened. They had shown an incredible kindness—even to us, the old enemy—which still amazes me even to this day.

I sincerely appreciated their generosity and signed a promissory note. In addition, two doctors created a travel plan in the United States for me. Fulbright provided air tickets to other locations in the United

States, so the interns who passed the exam were very excited about their first flight.

On the other hand, my plan, created by doctors who also offered me 500 dollars, had painted a totally different picture. I was scheduled to travel from Japan to the West coast by sea (sea fare was also 300 dollars). The rest of the trip consisted of me using an unlimited 100-dollar Greyhound Bus pass to travel through various places in North America, then finally to my destination. Across the West coast to Baltimore, the bus ride would allow me to experience America for 10 days, to meet and talk to people, to visit famous spots, and to enjoy the ride. Because once I started working as an intern, and once I was assigned as a surgical resident, I would not be able to afford to spend any time on such activities.

The plan and travel advice were detailed and extensive to an extent that surprised me. "The Greyhound Bus offers unlimited rides for one month after purchase of the ticket. As for a place to stay, the YMCA can be found anywhere, so search for it and make a reservation beforehand. The YMCA offers continental breakfast free of charge. For dinner, Chinese food can be easily found at a great price in any town in the United States." I had no idea at all what to expect, so I had jotted down every single piece of advice.

On May 17th, I received a ticket to the Mitsui OSK Line's, *Panama,* a vessel from Yokohama, as well as a check that amounted to 200 dollars to be exchanged in Los Angeles. The doctors even held a farewell dinner party for me. Suddenly, I worried that I might be showing terrible inconsideration by travelling to

America with my own money while my parents were suffering under enormous debt.

I could not think of any other way but to deceive my family. I told my parents not to worry, because I had been granted a travel fund from Fulbright. It was the best I could have done at that time. I thought there would be no chance like this available again. I felt bad about deceiving my parents and others, but my mind was set to take the risk of a lifetime.

One month later, the national exam was waiting for me. I had completed the internship at Yokosuka in March; however, I needed to determine where to stay and prepare for the exam. Luckily, Dr. Mohri offered me a space to stay and study for the exam, so I once again gratefully took up the offer.

I managed to survive the written exam. As for the oral exam, Dr. Minoru Ooi at Jikei University School of Medicine, was my examiner. I had a good start. Then the last question was, "In treating a gastric ulceration or duodenal ulceration, we thought the stanching was successful. Then, suddenly we were faced with recurrent bleeding, sometimes severe enough to interfere with the procedure. What could have been the reason behind this bleeding?" I thought of some cases like this from my time at Katakura Clinic; however, I was unable to articulate my response. Worse yet, English phrases that I had learned and used for over a year such as "I think" and "I believe" kept slipping from my tongue. My face turned red when the doctor said, "That terminology does not exist." I thought I had failed.

But he continued, saying, "the bottom of the ulcer is shaped like a net. So, blood can pass even after a seemingly successful stanching." I had become careless about the results of the national exam. For a second, I worried about the negative impact of lowering the passing ratio of Chiba University. But from then on, my mind was preoccupied with all but only the trip to the United States.

And after I had been in the United States for a month, I was told that I passed the exam after all.

Chapter Seven

My Travels to Baltimore, Residency at Saint Agnes Hospital as a General Surgeon, and Marriage

As my mother, younger siblings, and friends all saw me off from Yokohama Port, I felt the second half of my life truly begin. The sight of Mt. Fuji beginning to gradually grow smaller made it difficult to hold back tears. But I quickly snapped back into reality to concentrate on my hopes and life in America.

The ship I was on was both a cargo and a passenger ship that housed only 14 other passengers, so all of us were treated like first-class passengers. The captain of the ship and the other Americans on board taught us things like English phrases, how to greet and how to use a fork and knife. Due to their kindness, I did not feel lonely throughout the entire 12-day eventless journey over the Pacific Ocean. When I look back on this, I realize that I haven't made a trip on this scale since. It was truly a valuable experience.

After we came ashore safely in Los Angeles, I was able to withdraw American dollars from a bank, buy a Greyhound ticket immediately, and book a room at the local YMCA. I looked up the bus routes and places of interest in the United States to spend the rest of my money wisely on sightseeing as much as possible. Of course, I sent Dr. Holljes a message to let him know that I had arrived in the US, and to pass along my travel plans. Both the doctor and his wife were very glad to hear the news.

My plan was to go to Yosemite National Park and the Grand Canyon, then through the Rocky Mountains and Kansas on the way to Chicago, where I would stay with a senior classmate of mine from university. Then, I would head to Baltimore through Detroit. During my travels, I was touched by the kindness of the American people in the 1950s. Because of their kindness, wherever I went, I never felt anxious or in danger. I was a fish swimming in unfamiliar territory, but America's water suited me and gave me confidence.

At the Grand Canyon, a Native American chief told me that I was "not a Japanese but a native American," then forced me to take a trip to the bottom of the canyon with his son on a donkey-like creature called a mule, which greatly surprised me. However, I will never forget the sight of the moon and a million stars soaring over the cliffs as I looked up from the bottom of the canyon. All of a sudden, I remembered how I was a master at giving nicknames to my friends during the years in Yokosuka. I recalled several of those names: Mr. Miyai "Kumosuke" (a general name during the Edo Period that describes a laborer who does not have a fixed address), Mr. Yamauchi "Hikaru Genji" (the main character of the oldest Japanese fiction written in the Heian Period), Mr. Morikawa "Harudanji" (a name of a performer of a traditional comical storytelling). Now I gave myself the nickname, "Indian Chief, Crazy Horse," and I couldn't stop the wry smile that spread across my face. The chief let me stay in his house for the night, and in the morning, I headed for Chicago.

On the long bus trip, we passed through the Rocky Mountains, which I had always wanted to see. I admired the beautiful peaks while I could. Going through Kansas, I saw Angus cattle grazing along both sides of the highway. I was amazed that this sight continued for one or two hours along the road.

When I arrived at a hospital in Chicago, I visited a famous slaughterhouse and saw several hundred cows walking in a line towards the factory, waiting. It was at this sight that I realized just how big America was—on an entirely different scale than I was used to. I was also amazed at how ornate the buildings were in Chicago. They were orderly and tidy, but also elegant and lofty. The next day, my bus and I continued eastward toward Baltimore. At that time in Japan, there was a book called, "Let's Take a look at Everything!" by Minoru Oda; in America, I felt more like "Let's Do Everything!"

Now that I know more about it, I can introduce my readers to Baltimore. The eastern part of the United States began its history as the Europeans migrated to the region. At the beginning of the 19th century, a war between the Americans and the British began. This was known as the War of 1812. The war spread to Baltimore in 1814 and it was at Fort McHenry, just outside of the City of Baltimore, that the last and final battle was fought against the British naval fleet, with the Americans claiming victory. Francis Scott Key wrote the famous lines, "whose broad stripes and bright stars, through the perilous fight," during the twenty-five-hour battle, and these words later became part of the U.S. National Anthem. From this small port, a railway was built to the Midwest, and from there, US cities grew as more European immigrants came in to settle. Baltimore is the birthplace of the famous Babe Ruth.

In medicine, Baltimore is where the Johns Hopkins University medical school opened its hospital in 1889 and began its program of European-style medical education. Hopkins became America's first modern medical college, and it has trained a great number of America's leading physicians. Among these, the big names like Dr. William Osler, in internal medicine, and Dr. William Halstead, in surgery, undertook the education and guidance of those who entered their residencies after completing their intern training. Various surgical procedures were also named after Dr. Halstead.

Saint Agnes Hospital, where I did my internship, began the second oldest surgical residency system in the United States after Johns Hopkins. The program was established in 1906 by Dr. Joseph Colt Bloodgood, who was known as Halstead's right-hand man.

All of this prestigious history made me somewhat nervous. Saint Agnes Hospital was built inside the city of Baltimore in 1862, but later moved to its western outskirts. Thus, it is in a contrasting location relative to Hopkins, which is on the eastern side of the city. We could see the Baltimore harbor from the high hill we were on, and I recall Dr. Holljes said that it resembled the streets of Yokohama.

The University of Maryland and its hospital are also located in Baltimore. In order to save precious time in treating shock-trauma emergencies, around 1962 the University of Maryland Hospital established the first and famed department where patients could be transported by helicopter. Dr. Kazuhiko Maekawa (who later became a professor at Tokyo University) came from Japan to train there.

To return to my own story, Dr. Holljes and his wife greeted me most warmly, and after showing me around the city by car, took me to Saint Agnes Hospital and introduced me to Sister Denise, the hospital director. Sister Denise told me that I was the first Japanese intern at the hospital and called over a few doctors to give me various instructions. Even though I had arrived at the hospital three weeks early, she went out of her way to provide me with a number of conveniences around the hospital, which included the use of the intern residences and cafeteria.

She even gave me extra special treatment, saying that I could begin making rounds with the current interns at any time. This was all thanks to Dr. Holljes, so I once again expressed my appreciation to him. I was thankful for being blessed with such a great start in a new world, and I promised myself I would someday be able to return the favor.

Becoming an intern is the first step to being a doctor in America and means that one's medical school grades and recommendations are taken seriously. University hospitals select only the most superior students who rank first or second in their classes. I knew from the start that superior students would come even to a famous non-university hospital like Saint Agnes.

I shuddered with excitement when a total of eight interns including myself became acquainted with each other for the very first time on July 1st. Four American interns were the most brilliant and diligent of the group. The other four interns, including myself, were foreigners coming from Japan, Germany, Turkey, and the Philippines, which made us a rather diverse group. I felt that the other three foreign interns were like mighty warriors with strong recommendations from their medical schools.

Although I had already completed a year-long internship, I was quite behind in my studies, and my beginner's English was an immense handicap for me. As time went on, I struggled a great deal because of this. Surgery and internal medicine at Saint Agnes were far more challenging than at Yokosuka Naval Hospital, and we worked from morning into the night. I paid careful attention to each and every word that I heard, listening for anything I didn't understand to guard against making mistakes. Because of this, it seemed that it took two to three times longer for me to understand my work than any of the other interns. I frequently had to ask people to repeat what they said. I felt like I was playing a game every day to pay for not learning the language enough while living by myself as a medical student for four years.

My language barrier was especially challenging in the emergency room, though it became my specialty in later years. In those days, I was often protected by the American intern I was paired with. I gradually became used to the work, and little by little, it became more enjoyable. At that time, my partner and I would not have imagined that we might someday become presidents of the medical staff at Saint Agnes Hospital. Unlike Japan, in the US, doctors can open their own practice and they can send their patients to a specialist or a certifying physician in a hospital. But at that time, I gladly worked collaboratively with the other interns.

Although it was supposed to be a competition, we worked in a friendly environment and I was gradually becoming more and more recognized by the people around me. The work was very hard, and I feel that true to reputation, the life of an American intern is the most difficult throughout the medical career. If time permits, the first priority is sleep. The second is to eat as much as you can, when given the time to eat. Two of us interns were married at that time, and of course marriage involved managing an interpersonal relationship on top of all this sleep-deprivation, hunger and hard work, so it was very challenging.

Now I had to consider an area of specialization—surgery, for example—and compete for a spot as a resident in that specialty. I carefully considered which specialty would be best for me. It was generally said in those days, that becoming a surgical resident (general surgery, required a 4-year residency) was next to impossible. There were many applicants from those who completed their internships, and I was nervous about whether or not I could compete with the Americans.

Moreover, unlike the Japanese system, the American resident training was a strict pyramid system in which

10 people were accepted in the first year, and from there, only four could go on to become second year students. The others would have to become specialists other than surgeons—perhaps orthopedists, ENT's, anesthesiologists, etc. For third-year students, the surgery residency becomes a competition between two or three people in which only one would become the chief resident. In other words, the American general surgeon training system produces a single new surgeon per hospital each year.

In the United States, surgeons are given the privilege of starting their own practice, and by sending their patients to the hospital, they carry the big responsibility of both surgery and education. (In Japanese surgery as I understand it, any resident can open their own practice after two or three years of training.) And so, at a university hospital in Japan, I remember that medical students like us would follow 30 to 40 residents who followed a professor during the professor's rounds-visit.

America's strictness made me nervous. Meanwhile, even as we worked hard at our six-month internship, we had to find a residency that would allow us to fulfill our ambitions in our preferred specialties. I was thinking about going to Baltimore City Hospital, which was directly managed by Johns Hopkins, but I was informed that I could stay at Saint Agnes and apply for a surgical residency there. I didn't know if my efforts during my one-year internship at Saint Agnes were appreciated, but I accepted the suggestion because I believed I could survive the familiar place for another year.

At that time, the surgery department at Saint Agnes began its residency with six people. There were two Americans and four others, including me. We had all finished one-year internships with excellent grades and wanted to become general surgeons. I already felt, "it's do or die!" And not the next four years, but only the first year would determine if I lived or died. Now the days of headaches returned, as I worried about how to cover up my lack of education and training, along with poor English and inexperience.

I had just one strong point, which was the fact that I knew everybody at the hospital very well. However, there was no reason to depend on that. The residents who had just started had rounds and operations in the mornings, and there were lectures from the upper-level residents or outside professors in the afternoons. While doing rounds, we had to write daily reports for the patients who had been assigned to us and received instructions. We were also placed on duty every-other night. There were constant nighttime emergency cases and other things such as operations, and this led to days without any rest. I felt it was necessary for me to exert four times the ordinary effort to keep going—twice the effort for my lack of education, and twice again for my poor English.

When I had time off, I went to bed early. Any other time off, flew away with things like doing laundry, getting haircuts, and writing letters. I wasn't able to go see my favorite baseball games at the stadium. However, I gradually became used to the lifestyle of those frantic days. Little by little I found my mental space, more so than during my time as an intern, and so

I felt I was able to handle the reports of my patients much better.

It was a little after mid-December, as I was making rounds in the orthopedic unit of the hospital, when a professor visiting from Johns Hopkins asked, "Is there anyone who can take off from the residency to go to New York for three days from December 26th?" That professor was the head doctor for the football team in Baltimore, and was recruiting five or six assistants among the residents at local hospitals to help treat injuries or broken bones during games.

There were many senior residents who usually responded with delight, but this time nobody could go due to their schedules or their wives' schedules, and I was the very last person to be asked. Looking at my schedule, I saw that I would be able to take a break on either Christmas or New Years, but I knew nothing about football. However, my desire to see New York was great, so I accepted.

A total of five doctors left Baltimore for New York on the morning of the day before the game. There, at the (now former) Yankees stadium, we assembled with the team, and came out onto the field. The seats were completely filled, and the nervousness (as well as the heavy equipment I was carrying) made my knees shake and kept me planted where I stood. As soon as the game started, I was so involved in treating Baltimore Colts players with injuries and sprains, that I could not pay any attention to the game itself.

The only thing I knew was that Baltimore had scored a field goal with sixteen seconds left on the clock, tying the score and sending the game into overtime. The day was cold, and the entire audience wore hats, jackets and scarves. Even the players would huddle up against the heater during breaks. Baltimore was able to win the 1958 NFL Championship Game against the New York Giants after scoring a touchdown with the final chance they were given, and for a long time, that game was considered the best in football history.

This marked the beginning of my fascination with American Football. In spite of my ignorance, curiosity got the best of me, and I found myself asking the professional players around me what a "first in ten" is. They probably laughed at me, but even without knowing these rules, my fascination in football now exceeded my previous interest in baseball. Ever since that game in 1958, I have been a diehard fan of the Baltimore football team, now called the Ravens.

Since 1958 was the most important year of my life, I must take special note of it. This was because in the beginning of June, I met the woman who would become my wife. The afternoon of that day, I was suddenly called over by the hospital's pathology chief doctor. As soon as I entered the doctor's room after assisting a surgery, I was introduced to a woman. She was a second-year student at Goucher College, in the suburbs of Baltimore, and had come to the hospital searching for a summer job. She was majoring in chemistry and aspired to do work in blood examinations so she applied for a job at Saint Agnes, and was hired immediately by the chief pathologist.

But there was a catch. Her boss said "Mindy (her real name was Mineko, but he called her Mindy), you have a job and a husband." He then called over a clueless me and said "Tojo (this was a nickname he had given me) this is Mindy. You marry her." Because of this introduction, I was able to chat a little with Mindy. During that summer, I would see her around at work, but we did not have much chance to speak to each other.

But gradually, I learned more about Mindy. She was born in the Bronx, New York City, and was the oldest daughter of a family of four. Her father was a second-generation Japanese American, born in Brooklyn, while her mother was a second-generation Japanese American, born in Manhattan, who nevertheless had spent her childhood in Japan. (The name for people like this was 'Kibei Nisei'.) She had returned to America when she was 19 years old, so she was a Japanese-speaking American.

Her family's first generation had come to the East Coast around 1875 and settled in New York. They were illegal immigrants who hadn't settled in Hawaii or California on the West Coast, but instead settled along the Atlantic. They originated from Yamaguchi and Fukuoka Prefectures, respectively, and it was thought that they may have been influenced to move by Yoshida Shoin, one of Japan's most distinguished intellectuals from the Chōshū Domain in the Edo Period.

All of this meant that Mineko fell into the rare demographic of those who consider Japan their native country, having learned Japanese from their mother, while being completely American. She spoke in halting Japanese, but her temperament was definitely Japanese, and I felt that there was something powerful inside her heart.

Every time I met her, I got to know her better. First, she was four years younger than me. Second, when she was twenty, she got married but divorced after one year of marriage. At the moment, with the help of her parents, she was raising her two-and-a-half-year-old son at her family home. She told me that she planned on becoming a doctor, so she was studying in college with a focus on chemistry. She knew I was one of the busiest people in the hospital trying to establish my career, and regardless of the fact that she, too, was overloaded with work, she helped me with outlining and getting the main points of my presentations and perfecting my English pronunciation. She was a life-saver.

I managed to pass my first year of residency and become a second-year through a tough screening in July of 1959. From around that time, to achieve my dream—to become a general surgeon in America—I believed (rather selfishly) that Mineko was a necessary partner for me. And, unexpectedly, the urge to raise her child as my own began to grow within me. Yet I was very self-absorbed at that time. When I asked Mineko to continue working at the hospital, but take a break from college to support me, she agreed. I promised her that she could return to college if I was able to open my own practice and be financially ready.

And that year, on September 19th, we got married at the First Unitarian Church on Charles Street which was the main street of Baltimore City. Mineko was a Protestant Christian, while I was born into a Buddhist family because my father was Buddhist. But my mother was something closer to Protestant. I myself was somewhat of an atheist, so after considering all of this together, we decided on the Unitarian Church.

On our wedding day, I became so nervous at the altar—even though we had rehearsed this—that I was unable to answer the pastor, and he said my lines for me. The next day, Mineko seemed upset with me and said, "I did not get married to you, but to the pastor," but then she laughed. I was able to get a three-day vacation for our honeymoon, but Mineko made all the plans. So that night, we drove for four hours to get to a cabin in the Poconos mountains, which was good.

But the next day, together with other newly-wed couples we went horseback riding. Mineko was actually very skilled, which surprised me. It was the first time I had done this in my life, and after being tossed around on the ride, I finished sore and blistered, and it was horrible. Regardless of this, the honeymoon was an experience I would not forget any time soon.

At the hospital, work became more rigorous and I was swamped with it, as I was assigned to teach the first-year-residents. My preparations to teach took twice or three times longer than usual. Again, I was reminded through grueling experience how difficult English was and how difficult listening was. In spite of this, I was given more surgical responsibility over time and became the first assistant for surgeries more often.

The first thing I did when I got home for the day was sleep. And on Saturdays and Sundays of every-other week, being able to laze around with everyone else was the best thing I could imagine. I began playing with my son, Muraji (named for Mineko's grandfather), and doing my best to fulfill the role of a father took everything I had.

Just like this, the rigorous sophomore year of residency came to an end. Fortunately, I was able to become a third-year student in July 1960, and have the opportunity to become the next Chief Resident. Around that time, I finally began to gain confidence in myself, and it seemed that many of the surgeons also began to trust me. Ever since I was young, I had had the experience of always being saved by others whenever I encountered any difficulties, so I valued the practice of focusing on my everyday work, which included frequently checking on patients, reporting to my superiors, taking care of the residents under me, and protecting families. And there was no shortage of troubles that year.

My hobbies were American Football and music that I always enjoyed, and I was able to memorize a few songs from operas I liked to listen to.

Then, on June 19, my eldest daughter was born and given the name Naoko. A long time ago, a friend and I had gone together to a villa in Shinano-Oiwake two or three times. Next door to the villa was the Aburaya Inn, where Tatsuo Hori lived. I was charmed by one of his books, "Naoko," so my wife and I gave our child that name. Now, as a father of two, I became busier than before.

Fortunately, Katsumi Miyai, who had been together with me at the Yokosuka US Navy Hospital after he graduated from Keio University, had become a resident at the pathology unit at Johns Hopkins University and he helped me by staying at my house. Every day after work, he returned home immediately, helped Mineko and our children, and drove out for shopping. He left two years later, this time for the University of Toronto. On the morning of his departure, Baltimore was hit with heavy snow. Our family shed tears and lamented over his separation from us.

In the spring of 1962, I was informed that I would become the General Surgery Chief Resident from July onwards, and I was sincerely grateful for Mineko's efforts.

Mineko had been five years old when the war between the United States and Japan had begun. To get work with the Dental Department of the University of Maryland in Baltimore (the first established in all of the United States), Mineko's family moved from New York to Baltimore. There were no Japanese people in Baltimore at that time, and during the war, Mineko was called a "jap." She was bullied horribly. In the emotionally difficult years before she became a teenager, she was frequently beaten and spit at. Often, she even had stones hurled at her. Despite this, she continually received one of the highest grades in the class. It was through this experience that she came to understand the meaning of hardship and, from a young age, developed a resilient spirit.

It is my belief that in those days there was nothing else that could be done. Mineko learned Judo from her father, which built up her physical strength and developed her self-confidence. Soon thereafter, the male students who had once bullied Mineko disappeared.

At that time, Mineko began to wonder in the depths of her heart why the homeland of her parents, Japan, and her own country, America, were at war with each other. It had caused such great harm to her entire family and cast doubt about the future into their hearts, creating wounds that even now vividly remain. Unfortunately, because of this experience, Mineko was never quite able to completely accept or love Japan even after Japan recovered from the war and people could get anything they wanted, unlike in the United States which had more troubles in later years.

I don't have any regrets about my efforts to ease her pain, and my efforts alone, but her wounds—from youth—inspired my sympathy. Together with this woman, I started my last and most precious year in service to the hospital. During this year, the hospital trusted me with day-to-day tasks so that I became a responsible and competent doctor who eventually qualified as a surgical practitioner. I spent stressful times that required all my focus at the hospital. I was very busy with preparing for each new day, even after surviving surgeries that tested my judgment and demonstrated my achievements as Chief Resident.

But I knew that once I opened a practice, I could not consult with other doctors. And I wondered if I could find someone kind enough to trust me—a foreigner, a Japanese who used to be an enemy and might become a competitor. I could do nothing but give myself a chance. I was in the mind-set of a saying I had memorized in the past, "Do your best and let God do the rest."

Chapter Eight

The Ordeal of Opening A Downtown Doctor's Office

I realized after starting preparations that opening a practice in a foreign country would be harder than I had imagined. After I successfully passed the licensing exam for opening a private practice in Maryland, I realized it was truly delightfully good luck that Dr. Holljes had introduced me to this hospital—where he himself had interned—when I completed my internship in Yokosuka, so that I could do the second round of internships in the United States before jumping into residency. In other words, if you do not complete an internship in the state in which you want to open a clinic, the law says that you are not even eligible for the licensing exam.

I was confident that I had passed the test—at least barely—but I had been unpaid since July 1st, 1962, and if I did not acquire some patients, I would truly begin to lose the means of my livelihood. A young American doctor lent me half of his small office in front of the hospital, but half of the office expenses, including a private secretary, would be my responsibility.

I received everyone's blessing, and this would become the birth of the first practicing Japanese surgeon in the United States. However, business was quiet, and my staring-contest days began: waiting for a phone call from a new patient. With only my wife's income, I would not even be able to pay for my malpractice insurance. I was troubled. These were the hopeless days.

On one such day, I became fascinated by a notice from the Baltimore City Medical Society. In the past, there had been quite a few of these sparks of hope for possible opportunity. This one brought to my attention that two months earlier, a private physician from the downtown African-American neighborhood had retired, and even though there were as many as 700 patients in his practice, they did not have a doctor to take over their care.

The notice was signed by the President of the Baltimore City Medical Society and the Superintendent of the Baltimore City Health Department, saying that they were looking for a successor, but had no physician applicants and were worried. I was not a family doctor, but I had a rotating internship for two years, and I discussed the situation with both my wife and Dr. Holljes, who did not discourage me from applying for the position. I could not "keep a stiff upper lip." I could only say "Well fed, well bred," and after I applied for the job, I got splendid thank-you letters from the president and the superintendent.

Meanwhile, my wife got together with our African American maid, and they found a run-down, old-fashioned, gypsy fortune-telling shop nearby. Soon, Dr. Miyai brought in some other Japanese doctors who were working at Johns Hopkins, and as the master carpenter, in what seemed like the blink of an eye, he had turned the old shop into a splendid, elegant office.

He did not allow me even to help with the painting, telling me that my surgeon hands were more important than anything.

When an article about me came out in the local news, a few African Americans came to see me in groups of two or three, curiously wondering what a Japanese doctor looked like. But I politely examined the patients who came and gave them their diagnoses and treatments, and little by little many people began to trust me. My fee of $7 a year per person for my more than 700 patients was a very low price. (At that time, the regular fee was $7-$10 per visit for new patients at a medical office.) This seemed to explain why no other doctors had wanted to come, and some of my peers had seemed surprised when I applied. But it was my first office in America, and regardless of the pay, I was glad to treat the many patients who also enjoyed coming to see me. So, I worked hard every day, and little by little I came to treat many patients.

Most black neighborhoods in the 1960s were poor, and the houses were in terrible condition. In winter, things like kitchen burners were left on for heat, and without adequate winter clothing, people were always catching colds. Medicine only was not enough to maintain their health for long, and I saw, for the first time the "other America" before my eyes every day. Even though my patients were poor, the elderly people would wrap small amounts of money in paper for me at Christmas and Easter. "This is for your wife," the people would say in kind tones, as they offered me fruit. As a doctor, I could not help but feel grateful.

Meanwhile, my surgical patients in the hospital began to increase little by little. Within six months, I became busy with surgeries and consultations, and I spent half the day in surgery at the hospital, and half the day as the primary care doctor of the black neighborhood. These were mentally and physically fulfilling days. This was in 1962, more than half a century ago. I thought it was truly lucky that I had been able to come so far.

In 1965, President Johnson issued his Great Society policies, and new medical programs came into effect: Medicare for the elderly, and Medicaid for the poor. The yearly $7 payment I had been receiving from my patients until this point jumped to $3 for each medical treatment, and for doctors like me, who specialized in treating the overwhelmingly high number of the poor and elderly, suddenly the remuneration became exceedingly good.

Thanks to this, I was able to improve my office a bit, as well as increase the salary of my assistants for the first time, and slowly get things on track. However, my prosperity lasted only for a short moment. From around 1967, America became deeply involved in the Vietnam War. I started to struggle to make ends meet due to inflation. France also went deep into the war and finally withdrew, even before the United States did. Every day on television, the president's face seemed to radiate distress.

Also, at my office in particular, black mothers and other family members would come rushing in daily. The sons of these families, upon their return from the traumas of Vietnam, would fall into drug addiction, and become completely different people from those their families once knew. They would demand drugs, and if there were not any, they would sometimes beat their own mothers and sisters. The days that I heard about these kinds of assaults and had to treat the resulting injuries began to increase. This issue was becoming overwhelming in downtown Baltimore, where there were many black neighborhoods. I did not have the power to solve the problem myself, but reported about it to the Baltimore City Medical Society, saying that if nothing was done, it would become a truly dire situation.

Although it was only the report of a mere general practitioner like myself, the Baltimore City Medical Society wanted me to present it in person. I was able to meet those from the board for the first time. Yet, at the time, I certainly did not think this was something that would determine my future.

All those in attendance were white, high-society doctors, and just two or three people knew of my practice in black neighborhoods. They urged me to make my best case with other doctors to take this issue seriously. In later years, this led to the "urban medical committee," for which I was appointed as the committee chairman, and this was my first job ever at the Baltimore City Medical Society.

On behalf of the committee, I addressed several black doctors at a meeting about what we could do as physicians. Everyone kindly gave their support, and our conclusion was to emphasize and focus on seventh grade middle-school students, and through education at school, hopefully prevent the further spread of drug abuse in society. The people of the local bar association, and the teachers in charge of health education in the schools came together with us, and we developed our talks about drugs to be included in classes at school.

In our discussion, the doctors emphasized the harm caused by drug abuse, the lawyers explained how children can be criminally charged just by transporting drugs for someone else, and the teachers provided educational guidance on these matters to students based on the pamphlets we created. These were used in formal classes every year.

This committee was doing volunteer work without compensation, and when we actually put our plan into action, the number of participating teachers was small. However, the number of teachers participating gradually increased over the years. It was not easy to arrange training for each teacher at their convenience and I struggled with frustration at the amount of time it took.

Nevertheless, I pressed on, and I think I had some success. At that time, race riots were happening frequently, and though there were many uneasy days, I was gradually becoming accepted in the Baltimore City Medical Society, and in consulting with black doctors, I came to feel that we could do something not just for the Medical Society, but for the city itself.

By this time, I felt my love for Baltimore, my second hometown, growing stronger every day. I experienced a sense of achievement for the first time, not just from working for patients, but for what I could do for society. Yet I still did not anticipate that this would become my greatest strength in the years to come.

In my other work as a surgeon at Saint Agnes Hospital, my career was on track and I began to be recognized not only by my surgical patients but also by various hospital committees with important responsibilities. Around 1980, there was a shortage of emergency room doctors, so external doctors like me were recruited for the sake of teaching residents. I even had to work the night shift, and now my days were divided by three different responsibilities.

When my first son was born to my wife and me, we named him "Zenji" after my grandfather. I shared his school responsibilities with Mineko but doing so meant that I had to study something new every day, which was a daunting task for me.

Eventually, another doctor joined me at my downtown office and shared the work with me. But my responsibilities increased as the number of surgeries, lectures, conferences and board meetings at the hospital also increased, and I worked on the weekends without any time to rest. I traveled with my family only once in 1967, for the World Expo in Montreal.

But 1970 was an especially hectic year. I invited my former teacher, Professor Komei Nakayama from Chiba University, Japan, and asked him to give his famous lectures on esophageal cancer at three hospitals including my own Saint Agnes Hospital, the Johns Hopkins Department of Surgery, and the Thoracic Surgery Division at the University of Maryland Medical Center.

By that time, I had been able to—by myself—search for and purchase a 70- year-old house on a small suburban farm. Professor Nakayama was happy for me. Two years after his visit to Baltimore, Professor Nakayama lectured in Peru. I well remember attending this event with my wife. I am still deeply grateful to this day for Professor Nakayama's recommendation from Chiba to Yokosuka, which made it possible for me to come such a long way to where I am today.

Back at Saint Agnes, perhaps because my efforts were increasingly recognized, I became a leader at the hospital and was given the job of managing more than 200 doctors who sent patients to us through the open system. I had been able to complete my tasks at the Baltimore City Medical Society, but now, in addition to managing everyday life, keeping an eye on medical ethics and running a business, I also had to maintain an overview of our hospital's present and future. This was a much greater responsibility than anything I had ever imagined or taken on before, and on top of it, I had to manage the American doctors. I felt a little fearful.

However, as I climbed up from a board member, to secretary, and now, the vice president, I also began to take an interest in business administration in addition to being a doctor and surgeon. Among everyday medical examinations, surgeries, hospital rounds and lectures, I came to have a conviction that I could do something by myself. When I think about it now, it was nothing other than a truly youthful confidence.

At home, I always had Mineko as my living encyclopedia. For example, I might say, "The topic of tomorrow's meeting is this, but since the summary of my explanation is this, I want to come in with this kind of explanation." She would suggest, "It will be clearer if instead you start with the talk in this way, since everyone will understand right away, and it would also become easier to debate." She helped me with preparations every step of the way, and both the main topics and my responses went smoothly on many occasions.

In addition to fulfilling my obligation to the internal affairs of Saint Agnes itself, I asked for opinions from outside experts on economic and community development, in order for the hospital to develop in a comprehensive way with the surrounding society to more fully accomplish its mission. Eventually I came to think that development in the neighborhood would also be good for the future of the hospital.

And for the sake of promoting this idea, I joined Dale Carnegie's course, and re-learned English, especially listening. Many people must have been surprised when a foreigner like me warned that Saint Agnes Hospital should not relax just because it was the first Catholic hospital in Baltimore; that societal change would intensify in the coming decade.

In 1979, I was elected to be President of the Medical Staff at Saint Agnes Hospital. The previous president had interned at the same time as me, proceeding to the Department of Obstetrics and Gynecology from the emergency department where I had struggled with my poor English. Like a two-wheeled cart, he joined forces with me and helped me.

Being the president meant another big job for me. It began at 7:30 A.M. with a meeting with the Head Sister, a position held by a Catholic nun at the time, where I was briefed on a number of things such as the status of issues at the hospital from the previous day, today's special plans and events, visitors, hospitalization of special patients, etc.

My daily routine continued as I undertook rounds, surgeries, resident conferences, and consultations with my surgical patients at my office. In the afternoon until late in the evening, I attended patients at my downtown office, occasionally held briefing sessions with the doctors helping me, and had a late dinner with my family.

My hospital job advanced smoothly, and fortunately, the area surrounding the hospital seemed to regain stability partly due to being a suburb of the city. The Vietnam War was over, but the country was not returning to that splendid America that I arrived in for the first time in the 1950s. The harmful effects of the war dragged on. We Japanese had already experienced this, so I was not especially surprised.

However, it turned out that something did happen to surprise me. I received a message from the mayor of Baltimore that he wanted me to come to city hall. This is what had happened: In September of the previous year (1979), Baltimore had officially entered a Sister City Agreement with Kawasaki, Japan. The Baltimore side wanted a committee to build a network of general citizens of Baltimore together with people of Japanese descent. After consideration, they asked me to establish this committee as chairman. I had never lost my strong desire to do something for Baltimore, so I took this as my chance, and willingly agreed.

I requested the city secretaries to contact citizens of Baltimore with ties to Japan, as well as Americans who took an interest in Japanese culture, while I reached out to second-generation Japanese Americans for support. Six months after establishing the committee, we held our first meeting. I still had heavy responsibilities as President of the Medical Staff, along with all my other duties, so I was also worried about having enough time for everything. I lightened my burden at the hospital by delegating my responsibilities and authority to board members and others, which ultimately energized the hospital as well.

My private practice was doing well at that time too, but when my children entered middle school and high school, my life was busy with one thing after another. My eldest son Muraji graduated from Johns Hopkins University; Naoko went from Carnegie Mellon with an engineering degree to a master's course at MIT, and my second son, Zenji became a freshman in high school. I could not catch up with my children's growing up, but once again Mineko somehow managed it all, including making both ends meet.

Around this time, I began to think that I wanted to obtain a new qualification when my position as president ended. I had heard about the Master of Business Administration (MBA)—a degree for an administrative manager to succeed in business. It was an unfamiliar word, but I had great interest in comprehensively studying the management, accounting and administration of a hospital as a doctor.

With my private practice, surgical operations, tasks as President of the Medical Staff, and duties as the Kawasaki Committee chairman, every day spun around like a top, and even though I was getting used to the burden, I paid extra attention to my patients, so that I would not make mistakes and things would not go wrong for my residents in training, etc. I did not ignore meetings with the board members, nor did I miss my monthly reports to various committees, and I was able to fulfill my year's worth of heavy responsibilities without a problem.

On my last day, I bowed to many people and was grateful from the bottom of my heart. I had built a particularly deep appreciation for the support I received from a number of Sisters, and certainly from the Head Sister as well. The taste of the steak I had that night with my family was extraordinary.

Now it was 1981, and I was the immediate past President of the Medical Staff at Saint Agnes Hospital, and as former president, I had to host a big annual dinner party, which was usually held in the hospital's large lecture hall. It included academic lectures by the famous attending doctors who worked at the hospital. This happened every year, but this year I suggested to the Head Sister that we should expand the event from the inside of Saint Agnes Hospital to the outside.

First, I invited a distinguished American doctor as a guest speaker, and we used a famous hotel in the city center as the venue. I especially wanted to invite the medical staff who sent patients to our open-system hospital to come with their spouses or friends, and also to honor those who had worked for 25 or more years to come to the stage to be awarded with plaques of appreciation from the Head Sister and myself. I worried that these were unreasonable, but the Sister agreed with all of my wishes. I shed tears; I was truly glad she believed in me so much.

On the day of the event, the guest speaker was the best in the world, Dr. Michael DeBakey, who was the chief of surgery at Baylor College of Medicine in Houston. He was famous for vascular surgery. Our venue was the Baltimore Convention Center. The professor came in the afternoon the day of the event and completed his preparations. The lecture was about various developments in peripheral vascular surgery, and fascinated not only the general surgeons, but also general practitioners.

After a splendid dinner, we began the second part of the program. Sister and I stood on stage and called out the names of 26 doctors who had 25 years or more of continued service to our hospital. With hearts full of gratitude, we awarded them plaques of acknowledgement with our two names written on them. Again, I gave Sister my deep thanks.

I believed that raising the hospital's profile at this event might help spread its reputation and give moral support to the patients who put their trust in the hospital. When we came down from the stage, several doctors' families rushed to us, some of them, weeping. Many people said things like, "My husband has not been publicly acknowledged this way since he graduated from medical school. Thank you," or "My father was actually surprised and scared to go up on stage," or "I am grateful," etc. To me they said, "Dr. Nakazawa, I remember your first day. I am deeply grateful."

My heart was full. Even now, years later, I cannot forget that night. The big event was covered on a grand scale in the newspaper and was acknowledged by other hospitals as well. It strongly established our pride in declaring, "This is Saint Agnes Hospital!" I was deeply grateful and have never forgotten that evening.

Already a quarter of a century or so had passed since my coming to America. I was able to manage my hospital job and administrative tasks, but my responsibilities as a private physician were enormous, and government regulations on doctors and hospitals became stricter and stricter. The Baltimore City Medical Society, the Maryland State Medical Society (MedChi), and the American Medical Association in Chicago were now busy with constant discussion on how to deal with regulatory changes. Fear and anxiety filled my heart as I worried about the medical associations gradually losing power and being watered down. I was especially worried about the future of young doctors.

In fact, my son, Muraji, had apparently also been worrying about his future and he left medical school, and worked to establish a career in business. He became successful as a businessman and I was surprised. At the time, there were quite a few children of other doctors who also went in a direction different than medical practice. To me, medical practice is a precious, sacred profession, and because I have always held the belief that there is no occupation as splendid, it was a little disappointing.

Now that I had been helping with the Baltimore City Medical Society jobs and had been able to complete a major job at the hospital, the feeling was growing stronger that I wanted to continue my service to society as a doctor at the Baltimore City Medical Society.

In the 1980s, I had moved up through positions of responsibility at the Baltimore City Medical Society step by step from board member, to coordinator, to secretary, to vice president. But each time we had discussions at the board meetings, I faced difficulty with my English. In Japan, both before and after the war, we did not even have discussions, not to mention study communication. Having to participate in English discussions now became difficult, and there were times I felt like crying, but somehow, I persevered. I read two or three communication books and worked to clearly express my own thoughts until I could get my partners to understand me. I concentrated hard on continuing the discussions. I began to see better outcomes of my perseverance as time went on. I made a serious effort to grasp what my partners were trying to say at the Medical Society meetings.

I wonder if we Japanese, when arguing with opponents, have a custom of frowning on building theories or valuing logic. In American households, since childhood, both adults and children enjoy conversation at dinnertime and occasionally more serious discussions as well. I think that this is how the ability to persuade someone is fostered naturally among Americans. What a difference from Japanese households' value of: "Don't saying anything while you are eating." But I found in my own household, even if the family was chatting noisily, I learned from listening carefully to discussions among my children.

Chapter Nine

Serving as President of the Baltimore City Medical Society and Other Important Positions

In the spring of 1988, I was entrusted with the weighty responsibility of the presidency of the 1,300-member Baltimore City Medical Society. In my great excitement, I became unable to sleep at night. I could not stop thinking about the things I wanted to accomplish as the first Japanese person in American public office. The day after assuming office, I began receiving congratulatory phone calls from people I worked with through my public office as well as friends, including the Mayor of Baltimore and the Head Sister of Saint Agnes Hospital. I was especially happy that the patients as well as other African Americans from my downtown office celebrated with me there.

I was now extremely busy every day, what with being the head of the City Medical Society, my own surgical practice, my work as a general physician downtown, and my work on the committee for partnership with the city of Kawasaki, which I will describe in the next chapter. I served as the President of the Medical Society at a monthly board meeting and attended other functions. I was able to succeed thanks to the support from all of the people around me through tough times.

In fact, the economic clash between the US and Japan was so severe in the 1980s that it was considered a "trade war." The Japanese ambassador to the United States even had to fly to Detroit to calm unrest in the city. Then, as the result of the famous Plaza Accord, there was an appreciation of the yen and the Japanese economy was now at a disadvantage.

Given my personal position in Baltimore, and the difficult situation in my country, I was left feeling a mess of conflicting emotions that are hard to forget. I even got a few hateful phone calls about the car I was driving. (It was a large Chrysler Town & Country.)

On the other hand, the number of students from Japan began to increase. More Japanese doctors started to come to the United States, perhaps none to be practitioners, but as research scholars, who planned to stay in the US for only a few years. People like me, who restarted their careers in the United States, were rather rare.

But my friends were always supportive. And in my final year as Medical Society President, it was wonderful to have an opportunity to express my great appreciation specifically to Dr. Holljes, in front of members of the society at the big annual party. I invited him and his wife to the party to express how thankful I was for the help that he had given me. I told the story about James Dean, my English "teacher;" about opening my practice downtown, and onto the relationship as wrestling competitors between Dr. Holljes' sons and my son, Muraji. I was clear that the fact I was able to make it in the United States was thanks to the kindness of Dr. Holljes. Because of Dr. Holljes, my heart was filled with emotion about the goodness of America and the warmth of Americans. I felt I had had nothing but good luck.

Two months later, I was elected Vice President as well as Chair of the Public Relations Committee for the Maryland State Medical Society (MedChi) at the state conference. If I could say one thing to younger doctors now, it is that physicians should consider what they can do for not only themselves and their patients, but also for the community as a whole. In talking to the physicians who belonged to MedChi, I always called attention to the fact that the community around us is also critical to the health of our patients, and I took pride in living by my words as much as possible. Now, this election created a lot of pressure on me to best use my new position as the chair of the public relations committee to contribute to the community.

Communicating my thoughts frankly, in the simplest terms would be crucial. If I wanted others to understand me and to work well for me, I had to listen carefully and understand everything in spite of my limited English skills, especially when I was asked detailed questions. Additionally, as vice president, I had to manage MedChi meetings in accordance with "Robert's Rules" of parliamentary proceedings, which was new to me. I had to learn how to handle items in a meeting agenda. I struggled with all of this, but I learned a lot and was able to get through it somehow.

However, I found that my original job as a medical practitioner was deteriorating, and my patient care was backing up, so I decided to resign as the chair of public relations and vice president of MedChi after the first year. After this, my prospects of being a future president of MedChi ended. A major difference between Japan and America is that in America, the professional duties of the city and MedChi are unpaid. The medical societies would pay for participation at the National Conference, but there was nothing else monetary. Since it was only an honorary position, there weren't many member doctors who volunteered as I did.

As the president of the Saint Agnes medical staff, I managed to carry out my professional duties, but I was still uneasy about my other patients getting appropriate medical attention. I wondered if I would be able to break this "bad habit" of mine of taking so many honorary positions, but the gratification I got from volunteering was hard to replace. And in these years, in addition to leading the medical society, I had big responsibilities with the Kawasaki and Baltimore Sister City Committee, which I will detail in the next chapter.

Chapter Ten

Chairperson for the Baltimore-Kawasaki Sister City Committee

In 1956, President Eisenhower had launched the People-to-People Program. He proposed an initiative to strengthen affiliations to promote friendship and direct contact among ordinary people rather than just government diplomats. Based on this initiative, prefecture-to-state and city-to-city "sister affiliations" sprang up all around the world. Our city of Baltimore officially became partners with Kawasaki City in Japan, which had commonalities with us, such as being a port city. This news was very exciting to me, as establishing a relationship with Japan was truly a new idea to me and this was the first time I'd had such an opportunity since moving to the United States.

The mayor of Baltimore was William Donald Schaefer, who had been elected four times, and the mayor of Kawasaki was Saburo Ito, who had also been elected four times. On June 14, 1979, the "Sister City" agreement was officially signed at Baltimore City Hall. I remember being convinced that the two mayors, who stood face to face, their eyes meeting for a second, were touched in their hearts by true friendship. Although this happened just after I was elected President of Medical Staff at Saint Agnes Hospital and was extremely busy with my new position, I managed to witness the initial step of a US-Japan friendship materializing for the first time.

Later, Mayor Schaefer asked me to launch the Baltimore-Kawasaki Sister City Committee as chairperson of the Baltimore side, to deepen the collaboration between the two cities, and propel future projects. I was very excited and made up my mind to give myself as much as possible to the society around me while I devoted myself to my work as a doctor.

The Baltimore-Kawasaki Committee consisted of Baltimore citizens as well as volunteers from the second-generation Japanese American and Japanese community. All were interested in the development of economic and cultural exchange between the cities. At my first meeting as chairperson, I assigned people to subcommittees for culture, economy, education, sports, and academics; I held monthly meetings at the city hall and maintained communications with Kawasaki City. I was 47 years old at the time. In 1980, the following year, I obtained an M.B.A. from Loyola College in the city and was appointed President of Medical Staff at Saint Agnes Hospital. Even though I was young and passionate, my days revolved around work and I only went home to sleep.

In 1983, our beloved Baltimore Orioles won the World Series of Major League Baseball for the second time (after their first win in 1966). The team was invited by Japan's Yomiuri newspaper to play in Japan in 1984, and I joined the delegation on the trip led by Mayor Schaefer. As it turned out, the game at the Kawasaki Stadium was cancelled due to rain, and Mayor Schaefer and Mayor Ito were only able to play catch at a hotel venue. Nevertheless, I appreciated every day of my role as a go-between for the mayors during their visit in Japan.

In 1984, in commemorating our 5th year, we received and installed a truly magnificent stone lantern from Kawasaki City and its citizens at the corner of Inner Harbor, the center of Baltimore. The mayor of Baltimore, the vice mayor of Kawasaki City, and the minister at the Embassy of Japan attended the ceremony, and I served as the master of ceremonies. In front of about 200 citizens of Baltimore, the four of us unveiled the lantern at the ceremony. I devoted myself to the event with all my heart as I felt truly grateful that the people of Baltimore, my second hometown, showed such warm support toward us Japanese Americans. In return, Baltimore sent Kawasaki a large sculpture made by Mary Ann Mears, called Red Buoyant II. We were very proud of this gorgeous artwork for not only Kawasaki citizens, but also those visiting Japan from Baltimore to appreciate.

For cultural exchanges, we invited representatives of the Omotesenke and Urasenke tea schools of Kawasaki City to introduce Japanese tea culture. They hosted a tea ceremony at the Industrial Hall in Baltimore, which was attended by the mayor of Baltimore and the minister at the Embassy of Japan. Tea masters offered tea to Baltimore citizens.

In terms of education, we decided to exchange middle school teachers from Baltimore and Kawasaki. Two teachers were selected from each city every September (one teacher in later years). The participating teachers would visit assigned schools, and those from Baltimore taught English at Kawasaki middle schools, while those from Kawasaki taught Japanese at Baltimore middle schools. This program continued for 13 years. Although the program is currently suspended for financial reasons, the Committee is working to revive it in the future.

Another important task of the Sister City Program involves a Boy Scouts group. This group continues as a subcommittee. For its 30th anniversary in 2017, we celebrated middle and high school members as well as Boy Scout leaders. Each year, the group gives courtesy visits to both mayors before beginning their own annual activities.

In this way, we have maintained our main goal, "grassroots diplomacy," under the name of Sister City. This 2019 will be our Committee's 40th anniversary. Our work has only been possible thanks to genuine support by the mayors and citizens of the two cities. We are now planning various events for the anniversary.

1986 was an unforgettable year in this work. That year, our Baltimore City Sister City Program was awarded the first prize from Sister City International, an organization that incorporates all the sister cities in the world. All of us were excited to hear the news and filled with happiness. I expressed my sincere gratitude to everyone involved. Baltimore and Kawasaki continued to make efforts and we were awarded the first prize once again in 1989 when we commemorated the 10th anniversary of our Committee.

I retired as chairperson after three years, and the next chairperson was elected by the nominating committee. Since then, as new committee chairpersons are elected every few years, I serve as an ordinary committee member to give support to the subsequent chairpersons. The current chairperson is the 12th to serve, and the committee will select the next leader in one or two years to maintain healthy metabolism. I can attest that each leader has done wonderful work and further developed our program with new ideas. I am filled with gratitude for all of them.

Now, Baltimore's Mayor Schaefer completed his four terms and became the governor of Maryland. The next mayor, Dr. Kurt Schmoke was the first African American mayor in Baltimore. We also had the honor of receiving great assistance from him. During those days, for the first time in the city, a group of Asian Baltimore citizens together with an African Baltimore group celebrated their traditional clothing and music by marching down the main street accompanied by brass bands from the city high schools. The participants received a round of applause, and they greeted the new Governor Schaefer and the new Mayor Schmoke who met us at the front of the stage. In a samurai costume, I marched too, leading a group of Japanese children whose parents were physicians at the Johns Hopkins Hospital. Looking back on the pictures, I feel a little embarrassed today.

In 1987, when I turned 55, I received a surprise letter from the White House. President Reagan had chosen me from Asian Americans nationwide, to attend a party at the White House celebrating Asia-Pacific Month in

May. I was astonished by this letter, and when I arrived at the White House that day, I was even more surprised to find myself among three other Japanese Americans, as well as some Chinese and Indian Americans who were all well-known.

Next to me at the party, was the wife of US Air Force General Chennault, the aviator who had tormented the Japanese military during the war. She stood out among the guests, and despite her age, her clarity of words and the speech she made were outstanding. I still do not know who kindly nominated me for this occasion. President Reagan said in his speech, "It impresses me the most that Asians are hardworking and cherish their families." His beaming smile is still with me in my heart. Although the President was not able to spend much time with us due to an urgent obligation, I was nevertheless struck by his gracious speech.

Kawasaki City continued to give us support after I retired as chairperson of the Sister City Committee. Both Mayor Takahashi and Mayor Abe, who were the successors to the late Mayor Ito, also came to visit Baltimore. I cannot express what an honor and encouragement their visits were for us. Also, we are all extremely thankful to the citizens of Kawasaki, especially Mr. Fumio Saito and his wife, Fumiko, for their generosity to our committee. In 2010, then Mayor Takao Abe appointed me as the first Honorary Goodwill Ambassador to Baltimore.

In 2014, I was unexpectedly awarded the "Order of the Rising Sun, Gold Rays with Rosette" at the Spring Imperial Decoration. The mayor of Kawasaki invited my old friends including representatives of the citizens of Kawasaki—especially teachers who had visited Baltimore and contributed significant work to the city, as well as those who formed and led a youth baseball team to participate in a friendly match with high school students in Baltimore—to celebrate my decoration during my visit.

2019 will mark the 40th anniversary for the two sister cities. We are now in the process of preparing for a wonderful commemorative event. I feel deeply honored and grateful, and I am determined to continue to give myself to the two cities and their citizens.

Chapter Eleven

Failures and Setbacks

I believe that I was able to come to the United States and progress forward one step at a time, thanks to the kindness of many people, my wife's support, and luck. I cannot forget everyone who supported me during the hardest times of my life.

Readers may disagree, but I would not call my stories successes. On the contrary, setbacks always plagued me, and I suffered from them. As I mentioned already, I was accepted to the Seijo High School under the old educational system, after only completing four (instead of five) years of middle school, and I felt on top of the world during my teen years, but when I took the entrance exam for the University of Tokyo, I failed spectacularly. This was like being doused with cold water. Overnight, I lost my confidence, and felt for the first time that I had hit an impossible wall. But I spent the next year preparing for another entrance exam, with the music of Beethoven's Symphonies as my encouragement. And during my six years at the School of Medicine, Chiba University, though I continued to have failures, I eventually learned the ropes, and overcame them one at a time.

After medical school and my internship at the US Naval Hospital, my failure to pass the Fulbright examination was another big setback. Those who passed received travel expenses. But among the four participants, I was the only one who failed. This was a devastating shock to me. I believed that my dream of becoming a doctor in the United States was falling apart. It was obviously impossible to ask my father who had failed in business, or my mother who was sick, to help me financially, and there was no way of securing the minimum $500 (the equivalent to $1,600 today) by myself. Fortunately, two US doctors provided me with the funds in exchange for a signed deed that I would return the funds once I started to make money in the United States. However, if the people in my hometown, including my parents, brothers and sisters who were suffering from debts came to know that I was going to the United States, they would surely criticize me by saying, "Where did you find the money to go to the United States?" Therefore, I falsely told them, "I got lucky and am going to the United States with the Fulbright scholarship." I ended up deceiving not only my parents and my family but also the people of my hometown. It was fully my idea and I still carry a sense of guilt to this day. However, I was not able to come up with any other explanation at that time.

Yet another big setback, also a consequence of my own mistake, came after I became a general surgeon. I have already explained how I opened my clinic in downtown Baltimore. I responded to the city's call for a general practitioner in an underserved African American neighborhood, and I was living every day with joy although my plan to be a surgeon was slightly derailed. I treated my patients with pride, but my choice adversely affected my performance on the surgery board exam in later years. Once one has become a surgeon through the approved surgical training, switching to another specialization—choosing to be a general practitioner in my case—was out of the question. It was not that I did not know this, but I felt I had a clear mission to work as a doctor for those who are sick and for the general good of society, and therefore took on the downtown practice.

But when I took the surgical board exam, I felt at a disadvantage. The exam for general surgery was very difficult, requiring not only written and oral tests, but also a reference letter from a hospital's chief surgeon. After completing a four-year residency, I subscribed to textbooks and journals, attended various seminars, and even took preparatory classes offered twice a year in various large cities.

However, because I was so busy working as the president of the medical staff at Saint Agnes Hospital, as well as for the Baltimore City Medical Society, and volunteering for the Sister City Committee, it was difficult to secure the time necessary to prepare for the exam. I failed the written test once and failed the important oral exam—before three university professors—three times within five years.

I could not obtain the certification of the surgical board. It was such a big shock that I was almost truly depressed for the first time in my life. I almost lost my confidence in treating patients. Yet many surgical patients continued to trust me and to see me without noticing my despair. My wife told me, "This is a true opportunity. Please make an effort to become a better doctor." And day-by-day, the deep scar in my heart started to heal. There is a picture of myself from this time, in which I look angry and in agony. As a lesson to myself, I asked an artist to turn the picture into a painting and I have kept it as a reminder since then.

Setbacks continued. The term of the President of the Baltimore City Medical Society was one year, but even this may have been too long for me. As a foreigner, having to mingle with a number of Americans, and moreover, manage them, required a tremendous amount of delicate attention. Conflicts at work and meetings within the medical society were completely different from those of my volunteer work.

Doctors are truly wonderful to work with when they share a common goal, but sometimes they can also be proud and independent, and it was difficult for me to bring all the members and directors to a consensus at the same time. I took great care and attention to prevent failure. And yet, though I gratefully received advice from many who supported me wholeheartedly, there were always a few who were not supportive, which was sometimes a burden and hurt my feelings.

When I was nominated for the Maryland State Medical Society (MedChi) by the Baltimore City Medical Society, I was appointed to be vice chair of the council and chair of public relations. I worked hard to learn many new tasks. However, someone started raising questions about the patient medical records I had prepared as a general practitioner downtown.

Members from a special committee of the Maryland State Medical Society came to investigate my charts, and I was summoned to a special committee to answer questions. For almost 30 years since the opening of my practice, the Baltimore City Medical Society had never received a single complaint from my patients or their families. For the first time since coming to the United States, I felt stabbed in the back.

The medical charts in question were mostly from my general medicine patients rather than surgical ones. I was confident that I had not done anything inadequate, but from an internal medicine specialist's point of view, perhaps they appeared careless. This incident was my biggest failure. I was told to re-train myself and learn how to prepare medical charts from the beginning. I followed these directions and went through the suffering and indignity of going back to the "ABCs" of writing medical charts.

I was heartened that at least one doctor from the investigation committee said, "Dr. Nakazawa's medical charts are so much better than mine." But since I had respect for a variety of committee tasks, having been the president of the medical society myself, I did not criticize or make any objection. I quietly complied with the order, and in the end, I was able to overcome this setback.

This incident did not hurt my work as a general practitioner, but rather gave me an opportunity to open a new life path. The saying, "the future is a closed book," is a true statement. There are many doctors who might get discouraged by such events and could suffer depression, or leave the medical practice, but I always remember the spirit of overcoming the Sanpei Pass when I was nine years old, and it encourages me to remember that, "a man's journey is a succession of falls." More than anything, I felt strongly that I learned to be aware of my limits. It has been long said that failure is a stepping-stone for success, and I have been able to overcome crises one step at a time with this in mind and by transforming negative events to positive ones.

Chapter Twelve

Drawn to Eastern Medicine – From Acupressure to the World of Acupuncture (Third Chapter of My Life)

In 1990, I was 58 and continuing my practice without much change. One day, a long-time patient came to visit and asked, "Doctor, could you do me a favor?" She told me that she had graduated from the Ohashi Institute in New York, with an instructor certification in acupressure and wanted me to become her very first student. Of course, I had known the words acupressure and acupuncture, but I do not think that I had thought twice about them. However, at that moment, maybe there was extra room in my mind since I had recently retired from some rigorous and important duties. I thought, "Well, why not," and became one of her students. She had three additional students, and I started attending her lectures and hands-on training in the evenings twice a week.

My first impression of acupressure (also called "Shiatsu") raised doubt in me, and I took the training lightly. But eventually I started to experience a lightness in my entire body, a relief of pressure on my heart, and I realized that I felt good and naturally positive after receiving acupressure therapy. I had a flash of inspiration. At once, I felt I might be able to help patients by combining my experience as a doctor with the power of acupressure.

Once my mind was made up, I needed to study as a true student. I proceeded from the beginner's course to the intermediate course, and two years later, I passed the advanced class, reaching the point where I only needed to receive training from Master Wataru Ohashi in New York in order to graduate from the program and become a licensed acupressure masseur. Since I was only able to set aside two weekends every month for training, it was difficult, but I managed to graduate from the course.

It was a joy to me to have knowledge in Western medicine and also training in acupressure, which is a part of Eastern medicine. My way of treating patients as a surgeon shifted so that I paid more attention to patients' inner status. There were quite a few patients who noticed my transformation. But I remember Master Ohashi telling me, "Dr. Nakazawa, I think that you will be the first and last doctor who will come to me."

Indeed, when I went to the Baltimore City Medical Society with my acupressure license and asked, "Can I display this license at my office?" I was told, "No way, this is not something a doctor should be engaged in. This is a pseudo-medical practice." They all seemed to be surprised to hear their former president talking about acupressure. I was disappointed, but I started to feel strongly that I had gained something significant. I also felt fulfilled that as an Asian, I was able to study Eastern medicine in earnest.

Eventually, the Baltimore City Medical Society let me know that medical practice and acupuncture would be allowed together if I studied and became licensed at one of the few medical schools that offered acupuncture courses. I thought, "This is it!" and applied for the acupuncture program at the UCLA School of Medicine. This was how I started a new journey to yet another world at the age of 62, in 1994.

The head of the department was Dr. Joseph M. Helms. Coincidentally, he had graduated from Johns Hopkins University, gone on to the UCLA School of Medicine, then moved to France. With his good command of French, which he had studied in college, he had received training for a few years from a well-known French acupuncturist who had spent extensive time studying Chinese acupuncture in China before launching his own American-style acupuncture course back in the United States. Many American doctors had started to study acupuncture under his teaching, and since his acupuncture style had immediate effects, acupuncture became so popular that it was finally incorporated into the university course.

Acupuncture was originally introduced to the United States in the 1970s, by Chinese doctors who immigrated from China and started their practice for Americans in California. At that time, American doctors were not able to comprehend their practice. By contrast, Dr. Helms' theory and practice was very systematic and gained the trust of many American doctors. In 1980, Dr. Helms established an acupuncture school for physicians at UCLA. After successfully graduating, students were given authorization to open clinics as acupuncturists nationwide, thus many doctors, especially those of anesthesiology, internal medicine, neurology, and pediatrics started to add acupuncture to their specialization and receive positive feedback from their patients.

With these doctors, Dr. Helms launched an association called the American Academy of Medical Acupuncture (AAMA) and hosted annual symposiums in different locations. We acupuncturists are now learning about new practices and research by attending its conferences. AAMA also invites well-known practitioners from around the world to integrate acupuncture and traditional Western medicine. Our AAMA journal has become one of the most authoritative to many in the world. The year 2019 marked our 30th annual conference.

Chapter Thirteen

From General Surgeon to Medical Acupuncturist

I was accepted to the UCLA program in 1994, when I was 62. I graduated in 1995 and was able to obtain the license immediately. I am now a general surgeon M.D. and a medical acupuncturist. My two-year study of acupressure was also extremely helpful, and I was quickly recognized by Dr. Helms and given the privilege of working as his teaching assistant. You never know what comes in handy at what point. I was amazed! I have also helped with tasks at AAMA, and at the conferences, I have even given lectures and demonstrations based on Japanese acupuncture that I had since learned in Japan. I have become involved with the management of AAMA, as one of its central figures, and have played a part of its leadership, assisted Dr. Helms, and devoted myself to resolving political issues.

In 1998, when I was 66, I led a group of alumni and AAMA members to visit Japanese universities with acupuncture courses, well-regarded Japanese doctors who were practicing acupuncture, and Japanese acupuncturists to expand our perspectives. I am especially grateful for the warm welcome by Meiji University of Oriental Medicine and Dr. Toshikatsu Yamamoto in Miyazaki.

The next task I took on was to create the American Board of Medical Acupuncture (ABMA), i.e. a special academic society of certified medical acupuncturists, authorized by the American Medical Association (AMA). I was elected the second chair of ABMA and found myself busy again. By this time, I had passed my downtown office on to a new doctor and had gradually transferred surgical responsibilities to younger generations. By 1999, when I was 67, I finally had enough patients to be able to make a living as a medical acupuncturist. I expressed my gratitude to everyone who had supported me over the years, and the fact that former patients still help me by sending new acupuncture patients humbles me every day.

In 2000, when I was 68, thanks to Yasuyoshi and Masako Mamiya from Hamamatsu, I was able to give a seminar on American-style acupuncture to Japanese doctors and acupuncturists, which was well received. This seminar became an annual event that has now been going on for more than ten years. It is a privilege to visit Japanese acupuncturists and learn more every time I go to Japan for the seminar.

In 2002, when I was 70, I was chosen to become President of AAMA. Perhaps it was because I was older now, but I felt that the tasks of this honorable academy, established by Dr. Helms a few years earlier, went relatively smoothly compared to my struggles as the President of the Baltimore City Medical Society. Harmony with others is always key, and as a foreigner, it is a real challenge for me to continue accomplishing the tasks required of me while managing American members. I was able to complete the term successfully, and now I can fully enjoy my days as an acupuncturist at my own clinic.

Chapter Fourteen

Lectures on Acupuncture for Japanese Doctors and Acupuncturists

As an acupuncture practitioner, I specialized in Helms-style "electroacupuncture." At the same time, I explored various methods of acupuncture and widened the range of my treatments by mastering Japanese and Chinese ones. Luckily, I had a lot of acupuncture patients to try them out on. I always examined which treatment had been invaluable to me, thus what was best for my patients, and kept in mind their well-being and happiness. I followed a basic treatment based on *four diagnostic criteria:* "Observation; Listening and smelling; Inquiry; Palpation." Next, I would conduct a pulse and abdominal examination, examine the patient's tongue, and check the whole of the patient before finally starting treatment. Treatment outcomes improved and patients were happy enough to keep returning for treatments. In this way, I came to have more holistic perspectives than before, as I made sure to communicate with their primary care doctors.

Before this time, general practitioners were not so interested in Eastern medicine or acupuncture, and the doctors who were actively opposed to it were not few in number. But after twenty years practicing in my own clinic, I gradually obtained achievements and growing cooperation from other doctors, through my patients' word of mouth. I also started attending academic conferences, hospitals and seminars, more actively. In

2009, I was honored to be chosen to speak at the famous pioneer lectures on acupuncture at Johns Hopkins University.

A desire to share my acupuncture practice with Japanese doctors in Japan began to grow in me. Luckily, with kind assistance from Dr. and Mrs. Mamiya in the city of Hamamatsu, I had a great time doing so with interested doctors from all over Japan. I provided them with lectures, let them practice with patients, and led discussions. Many of the patients who participated had long histories of suffering, so we asked them to tape record their complaints in advance so we could prepare. I held several question-and-answer sessions with the doctors in attendance so they could absorb as much as possible from this seminar. The content of the lectures and training was quite practical for them, since half of them had already added acupuncture treatment to their everyday care. Dr. Mamiya and others continued to contact the participants, after the seminar, in order to track their progress, and I am sure it was very tough work. Such acupuncture events have now been held for more than a decade, and I am truly thankful for Dr. and Mrs. Mamiya, and their staff members and nurses, as the conference's success has been the fruit of their kindness and the effort they have provided.

Chapter Fifteen

Joy and Reflection on Receiving a Decoration

It was 2014, on the lucky day of April 29th (Emperor Showa's Birthday), when I received a letter from the Japanese Embassy in Washington, DC on my reception of the Emperor's Conferment of Decoration. I was very surprised and thought it could not be true, but there were many reasons for its bestowment as described below:

Embassy of Japan
Press Release
April 29, 2014

Conferral of the Order of the Rising Sun, Gold Rays with Rosette, upon Doctor Hiroshi Nakazawa

On April 29th, 2014 (Japan Time), the Government of Japan announced the recipients of the 2014 Spring Imperial Decorations. Among the recipients is Doctor Hiroshi Nakazawa, who will receive the Order of the Rising Sun, Gold Rays with Rosette, in recognition of his significant contributions to the development of medical exchange between Japan and the United States.

- DECORATION: The Order of the Rising Sun, Gold Rays with Rosette

- SERVICE: Contributed to the development of medical exchange between Japan and the United States.

- NAME (AGE): Hiroshi Nakazawa (Medical Doctor) (82)

- MAJOR TITLES:

    o Former President of the Baltimore City Medical Society

    o Former Vice Chair of the Maryland Medical Society

    o Former President of American Academy of Medical Acupuncture

    o The first Chairman of the Baltimore-Kawasaki Sister City Committee

    o Medical Doctor

- ADDRESS (NATIONALITY): Maryland (Japan)

Doctor Nakazawa has tremendously contributed to the medical exchange between Japan and the United States. He was the first Japanese to ever become a president of a city's medical society (City of Baltimore), and he also became Vice Chair of the Maryland State Medical Association. This contributed to widening the role of Japanese medical practitioners in the United States.

Furthermore, from 2007, Dr. Nakazawa became President of the National Acupuncture Medical Association (AAMA). Because of Dr. Nakazawa's active contribution, he opened doors for more and more Japanese medical practitioners to be able to proactively play a part in the United States.

For a long time, Dr. Nakazawa has been active in volunteer work as well. He was given an award in 1987 from President Ronald Regan (an award for outstanding Asian Americans who contributed to society). He also received a volunteer award from the Maryland Medical Association in 1989. He has also received the Foreign Minister's award for the contribution of promoting Japanese societal status in the United States from Foreign Minister Yoriko Kawaguchi in 2004.

Dr. Nakazawa has also played a large role in promoting grassroots exchange between the two countries, by becoming the first Chairman of the Baltimore-Kawasaki Sister City Committee. In 2010, he became the "Honorary Goodwill Ambassador of the City of Kawasaki" to the city of Baltimore. Now he is contributing to the exchange between the two cities as an advisor to the committee.

When I reflected on the explanation of this award, I recalled that ever since I had moved to the United States, I have always deeply desired to promote good Japan-U.S. relations and always considered how I could do that as a doctor. To have this even slightly recognized was a sincere joy for me. I cannot express enough how well I was taken care of and assisted by numerous people over more than six decades in America. I am sure there were more than a few people I inconvenienced. I am nothing but incredibly lucky to have come this far despite being a country boy, imperfect, full of holes, and struggling considerably with English. I begin every day by reflecting that the reason I have come this far is because of all the help from the people surrounding me.

In particular, I owe so much to my wife, Mineko. 2019 marks our 60th anniversary. She has always been my guide and ferryman leading me in the right direction and always kindly paying great attention to what I do so I would not go amiss. When I came to the States, I was told by a Nisei (second-generation Japanese immigrant) friend, that the second and third generation of Japanese immigrants—Nisei and Sansei—are like bananas, meaning, "they are yellow on the outside, but their inside is white and they think like Americans." But Mineko is different. Though she acts like a white person and sticks with American ways of thinking, she has a Japanese conservativeness inside, which surprised me, but for which I am so grateful. I was a complete amateur when I spoke to her for the first time and made her laugh by telling her, "Don't worry, just follow me." But she did follow me and many years later, at the Imperial Court on May 27th, 2014, I, together with Mineko, was given the Rising Sun, Gold Rays with Rosette. I am truly grateful that such consideration was given to a Japanese who resides in America, such as I.

In addition to this, I was also honored with celebration parties thrown by my Kawasaki City supporters, friends, fellow acupuncturists, and the staff members from Mamiya Clinic. I also received a wonderful banquet from Ambassador Kenichiro Sasae and Mrs. Sasae at the Japanese Embassy in Washington, DC. Numerous participants, including my friends from the Kawasaki Committee, kindly celebrated us. I am truly grateful. I am committed to continue doing my best as a doctor for both Japan and the United States. It awes me that I have been given such undeserved awards from the Emperor of Japan, as well as one from the President of the United States. I am thankful for everyone's continued guidance and support.

Chapter Sixteen

A Plea to My Fellow Japanese, Especially the Young People

Finally, I want to make a sincere request of my fellow Japanese people, especially, the young people. Whenever I go back to Japan, I am so delighted to see that it has become economically great, but I can also see a little bit of its inside as one who has lived outside for a long time.

Is Japan really prosperous? How is its inside? This is an everlasting concern for me. During my visits, I think it is surely getting better and better and I think this is a wonderful thing. Especially as a person who knows the Japan of long ago, I definitely think it has improved. However, I cannot help but feel there is something missing, as a person who saw the times before all this improvement.

Above all, I miss the passion I remember from my own youth. We, the ones who had gone through the bustle and confusion after the war, were nothing but desperate to strive and somehow survived through it. But what about now? Being in the States, and looking at the young folks who are ruthlessly competing with each other—especially the international students from overseas—I worry about the young Japanese folks and if Japan in the future will be left behind once again unless more people go out to foreign countries, breathe the air outside, learn about their surroundings and make efforts to continue studying. I hear that not only the number of Japanese students going overseas, but also the number of corporate or academic exchanges is decreasing. Please, I ask you, young people, go out there into the bigger world, for both your sake and the sake of Japan's future, before you say Japan is number one.

I am now reading a book called *Ten Years in Japan,* written by Joseph C. Grew, a former United States Ambassador to Japan, and it depicts well Japan's trends up until the year before WWII started. History is frightening. Please start cultivating your skills at communicating with people from other countries and think about making efforts to prepare for the future, such as starting to learn English—especially English conversation—early. I am concerned that the danger to Japan not only comes from the outside but from the inside as well. Thank you for allowing me to voice my completely audacious ideas here.

Far into the distance, I always pray for Japan's great future.

Epilogue

I have often thought about writing the story of my 80 years in two countries, but I could never seem to tackle it. Fortunately, with many sincerely dedicated persons' assistance and encouragement, I was able to recollect many of my experiences.

First, I am indebted to the former Japanese Ambassador to the United States of America, Kenichiro Sasae. He has written a thoughtful, warm preface to this book. I also very much appreciate his kindness in supporting my writing.

Ms. Mina Seat of UMBC (University of Maryland, Baltimore County) has been the prime force behind the editing, retyping of the Japanese edition, and moreover, supervising a volunteer and professional translation team. This has been a hard task for me, but her team has worked diligently to achieve the goal. Ms. Seat was also able to connect with an excellent publisher in Tokyo, Japan. Without Mina's assistance, I know I would not have made the first step towards publishing my book.

Ms. Kiyomi Buker, the Social Secretary to the Japanese Ambassador in Washington, D.C. has been vital in assisting and promoting Japanese-American Friendship for some time. Kiyomi possesses a congenial personality and assists in all projects to assure their success. I am indebted to her interceding on my behalf by asking Ambassador Sasae to write the preface for this book. Kiyomi is also the one who introduced me to Ms. Seat.

Those involved with the translation work are (alphabetically):

Mr. Bob Buker
Dr. Shannon Cate
Mrs. Miki Hernandez
Dr. Tomoko Hoogenboom and her class
Ms. Julia Marcos
Ms. Shizuka Otake
Mr. Ken Seat
Ms. Mina Seat
Ms. Yukiko Suzuki
Ms. Maki Toge
Ms. Drew Trevelyan
Ms. Ariana Washington

For the publishing side in Japan, I express my sincere appreciation to:

Ms. Mika Nishide, president of Beethoven, Inc., Tokyo, Japan
Mr. Yoshiyuki Watanabe, representative of Sogo Igakusha, Tokyo, Japan
As a medical acupuncturist, I have served many patients including VIP's at the city and state level. I often think of the future of Japan and America and recall the old Chinese saying, "A small doctor cures disease, an average doctor cures sick patients, and a great doctor heals the country."

In Japan, during the 10th century, a Japanese acupuncturist, Yasunori Tanba collected and edited all available Chinese and Japanese acupuncture literature, then dedicated it to the Emperor, calling it, "I-Shin-Po" (Medicine-Heart/Mind-Way). This was the first-ever Japanese medical book. In this book, Tanba explained that in order to heal the country, one must cure the people and to cure people, the mind and heart must too be healed.

This has been my motto whenever I see a patient; I think of healing the patient's heart and mind and thus I am able to nourish and heal his life. If I can do this, he will be able to heal the country.

Timeline

1932 Born in Takasaki City, Gunma Prefecture, Japan

1944 Entered Takasaki Middle School

1948 Entered Seijo High School in Tokyo

1950 Entered Chiba University, Department of Science and Literature

1952 Entered Chiba University, School of Medicine

1956 Graduated Chiba University, School of Medicine

1956 Began internship at US Naval Hospital, Yokosuka, Japan

1957 Completed internship at US Naval Hospital and received a medical license

1957 Came to the United States and began internship at Saint Agnes Hospital, Baltimore, Maryland

1958-1962 Began surgical Residency at Saint Agnes Hospital

1962 Completed Surgical Residency and became the attending surgeon and medical staff at Saint Agnes Hospital and a member of the Baltimore City and Maryland State Medical Society.

Passed the Maryland medical licensure to practice in Maryland

1979 Designated by Mayor William Donald Schaefer to be the first chair to organize the Baltimore-Kawasaki Sister City Committee.

1979 Became the President of Medical Staff at Saint Agnes Hospital

1987 Honored by President Reagan at the White House as one of the outstanding Asian-Pacific residents for service to society

1989 Became the President of Baltimore City Medical Society

1990 Received a master's degree of Business Administration from Loyola College, Baltimore

1991 Became the Vice Chair of Council at Maryland State Medical Society

1990-1992 Attended and graduated from the Ohashi Shiatsu (acupressure) school in New York

1994-95 Entered UCLA, an extension of the Acupuncture School. Became a medical acupuncturist. Received a license to practice acupuncture along with surgery in the state of Maryland

2000   Began the AAMA Japan Seminar at Mamiya Clinic in Hamamatsu, Japan. This lasted for 15 years.

2006-2008 Chair of American Board of Medical Acupuncture (ABMA)

2008-2009 President of American Academy of Medical Acupuncture (AAMA)

Honors

2014 Order of the Rising Sun, Gold Ray with Rosette from the Emperor of Japan at the Imperial Palace

2011 Social Service Award Chiba University Medical School Alumni Association

2009 First recipient of the Saint Agnes Hospital Shrine of Healing Hands Society

2004 Honorable Ambassador award for friendship from Kawasaki to Baltimore by the mayor of Kawasaki City, Takao Abe

1994 Japanese Foreign Minister Award, citing effort in elevating the social standing for Japanese and Japanese physicians in the USA.

1989 Social Service Award from the Maryland State Medical Society

1987 Honored by President Reagan at the White House as one of the outstanding Asian Pacific residents

1985 Social Service Award from the Baltimore City Medical Society

1984 December 2, 1984 designated as "Hiroshi Nakazawa M.D. Day" in Baltimore by Clarence 'Du' Burns

Made in the USA
Middletown, DE
10 September 2022

10146809R00080